Acknowledgments

Special thanks to Rachel Chahanovich for her work on the cover design.

Special thanks to Julie Wendover, Christy Thompson and Tina Meehan for proofreading.

Dedication

My endorsements are from pastor friends who are not famous in the conference circuit but who spend their lives caring for the flock of God in local churches. These are the true unsung heroes, who are not afraid to challenge the lion and the bear to snatch a soul from the fire. They are not household names but their identity is known to heaven. They don't have a large following or bank account, but they have a massive heart for God's people. They are the ones who care for the 99 and the one who is caught in the snare. They don't always do it right, and sometimes they feel alone, but they keep on giving and loving even when no one seems to care. They are the ones who see the fruit of all the wild teachings and "apostolic" fads in the lives of the saints, and do their best to clean the messes. These are the ones to whom this book is dedicated.

Endorsements

"A timely wakeup call. 'They Call Themselves Apostles,' clarifies the true role of Apostles in a heart of liberating the Church to walk in her true calling and purpose. Hanley lovingly confronts *the elephant in the room* that few have had the courage or character to challenge. As a pastor, I have witnessed the worldwide Church welcoming in these so-called apostles without question, along with false teachings and delusions of every kind. In the name of 'unity' they are actually dividing up the body of Christ: *'I am of apostle so and so... and I follow apostle such and such. You're either with us or against us, align or be silenced.'* Hanley challenges believers to follow Christ in true love and freedom. No matter who you are, this book will shake and confront you, opening your eyes to the truth."

- Kyle Chahanovich, Senior Pastor, Banner of Love Church, Wicklow, Ireland.

"PJ Hanley has a great love for the Church of God to be in accordance with the Word of God. In this book he sets out a welcome and uncompromising warning to the dangerous doctrines that are being accepted by too many leaders today. This is a very timely critique for the sake of the Body of Christ. Within the pages of this work, you will find sound Biblical support, which serves to reveal the errors being embraced by the Church in many places. This book therefore, brings essential and much needed clarity that should make the reader think seriously about these issues, which are increasingly becoming a troubling trend in the Church. Have we reached the place where the Church is building without Christ, yet in His name? What are the dangers and how do we recognize them? I believe that this may seem a hard-hitting study to some readers, but given what this book reveals, that is what is essential to staying the course in Christ! It is effectively sounding a warning that is needed urgently but which many are afraid to do. It is time to stand against false doctrine by those peddling the Word of God and stand for the truth revealed in God's word. PJ encourages the Church to remain heavenly focused and take our eyes off using church for our own agenda's. It is a clear and concise book with a message that encourages the local church to fulfil its Biblical calling without excuse or apology to men. You will want this book to share with others.

- Paul Phillips, Pastor, Wexford Christian Community Church, Wexford, Ireland

P.J. Hanley has done a fantastic job of exposing an error that has developed into the Hyper-Apostolic movement. Ephesians 4:11-15 explains that part of the function of the true apostle is to equip the saints for the work of ministry …so that we are no longer children tossed here and there by waves and carried away by every wind of doctrine, by the trickery of men, by craftiness in deceitful scheming, but to speak the truth in love.

P.J. has diligently researched and studied this movement and has shown how these new apostles, many of them unknowingly, are indeed promoting winds of doctrine that are causing others to be tossed to and fro from the very truth they have been entrusted with!

I applaud P.J. for his tenacity and courage in writing this book. I pray that after reading this book many will be spared the pain and ruin of being shipwrecked on the reef of the Hyper-Apostolic heresy and error. It is a must read!

- Gary A. Smith, Pastor of New Life Christian Fellowship, Alpena, Michigan

Everyone wants to be an apostle nowadays! The word "apostolic" seems to be a major buzzword in modern Charismatic circles. Book after book, and sermon after sermon, all referencing their specific spin on the subject and, of course, Ephesians 4. As a child of the eighties in the Charismatic Church bubble, I have always been very familiar with the word. But I noticed some years ago that what we are now hearing has some stark and troubling differences. And when these differences are brought under the anti-septic microscope of Scripture, there is a clear and pronounced distinction between what the New Testament writers deemed an "apostle," and our modern version and theology of the "apostolic."

This book sheds immense light on this truly important Biblical topic. It exposes the man-made dogmas and brings forth from the pure lens of God's word, what a "TRUE APOSTLE" looks like. I know it did for me, and I believe it will do the same for you.

- Mike Hanley, Senior Pastor, Banner of Love Church,
- Port Ewen, NY

Contents

Introduction

I am privileged to have lived through two great revivals. I have seen the result of the Holy Spirit's work in the Church, and I have also seen the injury caused by false and abusive leaders. Indeed, it seems that every time there is a significant move of God in restoration, counter movements appear and hijack the leadership. Like vultures they ride in on the currents of revival, pretending to fan the flames, while they feast on the Body of Christ. This time however, it seems like the hordes of hell have been released, and this should not surprise us, since we are living in the last days. Nevertheless, those who are called to shepherd the Church in revival, are often unaware of the stewardship they possess. In a time of great joy and excitement, they tend to lower their guard. Like David who became familiar with victory, they take time out from the battle, and fall victim to a different kind of predator. In the same way, the current leadership of the Church seems to have been lulled into complacency, forgetting the need for vigilance and sound teaching. Preoccupied with their new freedom, and the message of the Father's love, they have become desensitized to danger, and sitting ducks for deception. Checking their brains at the door of experience, they have become the promulgators of every fad and trendy "message" that is "outside the box." Opting for political correctness, rather than Scriptural integrity, they ostracize those who disagree, labeling them as "negative" and "religious." Now, 20 years later, the fruit of this inclusiveness and "love wins but theology divides" remodeling, is apparent. A generation of rogue theologians has emerged from their ministry schools and apostolic centers. The Body of Christ is filled with confusion and heretical teachings, and still there is no repentance or sorrow or mourning. There appears to be no elder statesmen to stand up and issue a challenge, or a warning. Calling themselves apostles, they have abandoned the Church to the wind and waves of heresy, while they extol the virtues of tolerance and diversity. What blind guides they have become, swallowing both the gnat and the camel. Foolish fellows, who like Eli, have great stature and influence, but are raising wayward spiritual children. How much longer will you observe this recklessness and say nothing?

Folks, the Body of Christ today is in desperate need of leadership. I am convinced that there are many out there who see what's happening, but are afraid to speak up because of their alliances. But as for me and my house, we will serve the Lord and speak the truth in love, even if no one stands with us. We are living in a time of great sifting and testing. False teachings and full-blown heresies are spreading like wildfire, as the Church is being ravaged by wolves. There is a massive fraud being perpetrated under the guise of restoration and reformation. In this book, I have attempted to address what I believe to be the source of the silence. I have attempted to shine the light and expose the darkness. When pointing out the obvious to those who don't see it, one must be very specific. This movement is vast in scope and influence and the books are in the public square. There is no way to address the issues without quoting from them. I have mentioned names to reveal the source and the widespread nature of the teachings being presented. I have not done it to malign anyone or to suggest that they don't love Jesus. On the contrary, I mention names to call for repentance and to snatch as many as possible from the fire. I have spent much time dealing with the writings of C. P. Wagner because he was the father of the movement and the primary mover and shaper. I have no personal axe to grind with anyone and can honestly say that I want the best for all. I believe that when there is teaching and conduct among leaders that causes harm to the Church, those of us who are shepherds have a Biblical mandate to speak out. I realize that there are many who feel that we should never mention names, but this not a Biblical position.[1] Therefore, I submit this work to the Body of Christ for its careful review!

---

[1] 2 Tim 2:17, 3 John 1:9

Warning

Before you read this book, it is strongly suggested that you first read the Introduction on pages 9 through 11. There the author explains the reason for writing the book and mentioning the names of other ministers. It is very important to come at this work with the right spirit and motives. It is also very important to understand that reading it could rock your world! Sometimes there is a price to be paid for speaking the truth, even when done with much love!

Chapter One
Breaking News
Mankind Has Entered a New Apostolic Age?

If you read Christian books or visit the conference circuit, you already know that apostles are back and taking the Body of Christ by storm. Where there used to be pastors and teachers or prophets, almost all are now apostles. There are "nuclear apostles," "territorial apostles," "ambassadorial apostles," "Microsoft apostles," "workplace apostles," "marketplace apostles," "vertical apostles," "horizontal apostles," "presiding apostles," and "convening apostles." That's a lot of apostolicity! How did this happen you may ask? And what did they do with the pastors? Well it appears that while many of us were busy hosting the fresh outpouring of the Holy Spirit, or recovering from Y2K, a "New Apostolic Age" began. At least that's what they are saying, even pinpointing the year it became official as 2001.

"The Second Apostolic Age began roughly in 2001, heralding the most radical change in the way of doing church at least since the Protestant Reformation. This New Apostolic Reformation embraces the largest segment of non-Catholic Christianity worldwide, and the fastest growing. Churches of the Apostolic Movement embrace the only Christian megablock growing faster than Islam."[2]

There are, of course, apostles in the Church today. However, a "Second Apostolic Age" is another thing entirely. Such terminology suggests something comparable to, or even greater than the commissioning of the Twelve. These are

---

[2] C. Peter Wagner, International Coalition of Apostles.
http://www.icaleaders.com/about-ical/definition-of-apostle

14

stunning statements that shock and amaze. Nevertheless, something very significant is happening in the Church worldwide. A movement is underway that is radically altering the structure and focus of 21st Century Christianity.

"There is a global apostolic movement that is shaking Christianity and expanding the church as never before! This is an important shift away from the typical denominationally led church movements of the past."[3]

"I believe that much of the church in our day is making a dramatic transition out of denominationalism and into apostolic families. This is often referred to as the emerging apostolic age.... In late 2007, the Lord spoke to me and said, 'Mankind has just entered into the new apostolic age.'"[4]

Though there is "revelatory" flexibility regarding the date it began, in the last fifteen years this New Apostolic Reformation (NAR), as it has come to be known, has grown into thousands of organizations and ministries spanning the globe. It also appears to have been accepted as mainstream by most in the Charismatic and Pentecostal movements. This is not necessarily due to their knowledge of the movement, but rather its effectiveness in infiltrating churches and winning them to the cause. Also, the sheer magnitude of the group and the number of celebrity leaders that have joined its ranks, make it difficult for local pastors to question the validity of its claims.

Another reason for its stealth-like rise to prominence is its apparent looseness or lack of organization. Adherents to the

---

[3] *Earmarks of a True Apostolic Movement*, Joseph Mattera,
http://www.charismanews.com/opinion/the-pulse/48760-12-earmarks-of-a-true-apostolic-movement Charisma
[4] Kris Valotton, *Heavy Rain*, Chosen Books, a division of Baker Publishing Group, 2016

movement, and its various networks, appear to be speaking and acting autonomously while their affiliations are either unknown or downplayed. Being convinced that their "alignment" is merely relational, they find it easier and even Christ-like to follow the throng. Thus, the vast majority of Christians, and even pastors, are unaware that a large-scale movement even exists.

My Early Training

The only real challenge to the NAR so far has come from Cessationist[5] internet Heretic Hunters, who are mostly professional critics. To them, almost all the spiritual gifts and experiences of the Holy Spirit ended in the 1st Century, when intellectual knowledge and understanding appeared! Thus, they brand all Charismatics, Pentecostals and especially those of the Toronto Movement as heretics. Indeed, even Billy Graham frequently shows up in their list of apostates. Thus, whatever valid criticism they present, especially of the NAR, is hard to receive given their attitude and belief that apostles no longer exist. Consequently, the baby is immediately thrown out with the bathwater. Nevertheless, I am *not* one of those critics. I have been a Charismatic pastor and teacher for nearly forty years and a recipient and participant in subsequent revivals. I am a firm believer in the presence and power of the Holy Spirit in the Church today, and the restoration of the gifts and ministries that were active in the Early Church. My spiritual mentor majored on the theme of the restoration of apostles and prophets, and was instrumental in what were the formative years of the Apostolic Movement. I cut my teeth, so to speak, listening to and reading the writings of many who went on to be senior leaders. I've seen "apostles" up close and personal, and have lived long enough, and been through enough, to know the difference between the revelation of God's Word and starry-eyed Kool-Aid. I have lived

---

[5] Cessationists believe that the gifts of the Holy Spirit ceased in the 1st Century

through two great 20th Century revivals, and have a deep appreciation for the work of the Holy Spirit in restoring the Church. Therefore, I am uniquely qualified to critique the current Apostolic Movement, and analyze what it has become. However, before I do that, let me discuss the reality of apostles in the Church today.

Apostles are Real

"And He gave some as apostles, and some as prophets, and some as evangelists, and some as pastors and teachers, for the equipping of the saints for the work of service, to the building up of the body of Christ; until we all attain to the unity of the faith, and of the knowledge of the Son of God, to a mature man, to the measure of the stature which belongs to the fullness of Christ." Eph 4:11-13

This passage is frequently used as a proof text for the restoration of apostolic ministry in our time. With this I wholeheartedly agree. Paul clearly teaches that Christ gave these ministries as gifts to equip the church in its work of service. Nowhere does the Bible suggest that this was temporary. On the contrary, since we receive all gifts through the presence of the Holy Spirit, who is with us to the end of the age,[6] it is clear they were supposed to continue with us also. And indeed, they did, even in the Dark Ages, though they were scarce and rarely accepted. However, through the Reformation and the revivals of the following centuries, the gifts and ministries were restored to our understanding and practice. Evangelists, pastors and teachers were accepted early on, while prophets and apostles were not recognized until the latter part of the 20th Century. This indeed is the work of the Holy Spirit, both in its order and timing.

---

[6] Mt 28:20

Many Evangelicals, however, reject the idea that the gifts of the Holy Spirit are for believers today. They have been taught that these were only for the Early Church, to get them launched, and they disappeared with the Twelve Apostles. Thus, they say that apostles and prophets were only for that time. Yet they are inconsistent in their belief, as well as unscriptural, since they acknowledge the Holy Spirit is still with us, and evangelists, pastors and teachers also exist today. Why then is it so difficult to accept the restoration of apostles and prophets? To this they answer that prophets had to be perfect in their revelation like the Prophets of Israel, and that apostles had to have seen the Lord Jesus after His Resurrection. This, of course, is how they qualify Paul. Nevertheless, both arguments are false, since prophets existed in the New Testament who were not perfect in their revelation,[7] and apostles existed who had not seen the Lord after His Resurrection, such as; Barnabas, Timothy and Titus.[8] Furthermore, this does not in any way detract from the special calling of *the* Prophets of Israel and *the* Twelve Apostles of the Lord. These are the ones who laid the foundation of the Church, which is the knowledge of Jesus the Messiah.[9] To suggest that apostles can't exist today because Jesus chose the Twelve as His special emissaries, is to misunderstand what apostles are, and to contradict the evidence of the New Testament and the testimony of Paul. It is like saying that because God is the Perfect Father, fathers can't exist today.

Train to Glory?

Since the Holy Spirit is restoring the ministry of apostles to the Church, what could be wrong with a world-wide Apostolic Movement? This is an important question that, sadly, few are

---

[7] I Cor 13:9, 14:29
[8] Acts 14:14, 2 Cor 8:23 (The Greek word translated "messengers" is *apostolos*)
[9] Eph 2:20. (The article denotes that not any apostles or prophets are spoken about but "the" apostles and "the" prophets.)

asking. The majority seem content to enjoy the benefits without considering the long-term effect. What else is new? It's a moving train, promising glory, so they jump on board. But those who have suffered a few train wrecks are more likely to need some assurances. Having lived through the Discipleship Movement[10] of the late seventies, and been a "church government" junkie for nearly twenty years, I have learned the value of asking questions. Not all that glitters is gold, and moving trains can be derailed or hijacked. Indeed, Church history reveals the painful saga of Holy Spirit-initiated movements that went wrong, and heaven-sent trains that were derailed by carnal strategies. Therefore, it behooves every Christian, and especially pastors and leaders, to take a good hard look at the NAR (New Apostolic Reformation). Its formation, staggering growth, and popularity, and elaborate and largely secret structure, are warning flags of the derailment to come. It is my firm conviction that what started as a move of God restoring New Testament Church structure, was subsequently hijacked by men with larger-than-life egos, and grandiose visions of world domination in the name of Jesus.

Conclusion

Many years ago, in the early days of the revival, I remember a discussion I had with two well-known leaders. After a while, one of them looked at the other and said, "He asks all the right questions." I never forgot that statement, which I think was a compliment, and I also remember how I felt when I heard it. I felt strange and puzzled. What's wrong with asking good

---

[10] The Discipleship/Shepherding Movement was a well-intentioned attempt to bring Biblical government and order to the young Charismatic Movement of the time. It was an experiment that went awry and brought much pain and hurt to the Church. It was a forerunner to the current Apostolic Movement which, despite strong denials, embodies much of the same spirit and methodology. For more on the Discipleship Movement see the book, *The Shepherding Movement, Controversy and Charismatic Ecclesiology*, by S. David Moore available at Amazon.com

questions? What's wrong with questioning the goals and strategies of a movement? What's wrong with wanting to know if something a Christian celebrity teaches is Biblical or missing the mark? Are we to just blindly follow leaders and fall into the same pit? As time went on I realized what made me uncomfortable that day. My friend's statement was complimentary but it was also eerily final. It was as if he was saying, "It's the right question, but asking it will get you in trouble."

Dear friends, we are living in a time when asking questions, or challenging the claims of those in the Apostolic Movement, is akin to having one's credentials revoked and one's integrity challenged. Charges of "divisiveness" and a "religious spirit," or "legalism," will be hurled at any pastor or leader who ventures to question "God's Anointed Ones." As I write this book, I am aware that it could cost me some relationships. Nevertheless, as a pastor and teacher I have a responsibility to teach God's people and warn of impending danger. We are called to speak the truth in love regardless of how unpopular it makes us.

The teachings of the New Apostolic Reformation are not hidden; they are hugely popular and becoming mainstream. They are not being presented as queries to provoke thought or study, but as decrees, commands, and dogmas that are to be accepted and obeyed. Furthermore, elements in this movement are insisting that all pastors and leaders must "align" with their "counsels" and "roundtables" to be considered legitimate. These are very dangerous trends in the Church that need to be confronted and challenged for the good of all. Yet, as of this date, to my knowledge, there is no careful examination or critique coming from Charismatic, Pentecostal or Revival circles. That is the purpose of this book -- to examine the claims and teachings of this movement and compare them carefully with what the Scripture says. The time has passed for silence! Mature leaders who love God and His people should not be afraid to have their teachings challenged. On the contrary, if they are truly humble they will welcome scrutiny. Furthermore, those leaders who love God's people should have the guts to confront that which is damaging the Church and quit with the compromise.

I have no ill will in my heart towards anyone in the NAR. Many of them have been heroes of mine, but I am deeply disappointed in their willingness to sell out the rank and file to preserve their own reputations. I love the people of God and the work of the Holy Spirit, but I cannot be quiet about what is happening. I grew up at a time when Christian leaders cared enough to speak out about things that were wrong and potentially damaging. I remember when many spoke out about the errors of the discipleship movement. Eventually, they were listened to. As melodramatic as it seems, I wish to echo the words of Luther, "Here I stand, I can do no other, so help me God." It is my sincere hope that this short work will be instrumental in the lives of many pastors and churches and those called to genuine apostolic ministry.

Chapter Two
Culture of Honor?

"For, I think, God has exhibited us apostles last of all, as men condemned to death; because we have become a spectacle to the world, both to angels and to men. We are fools for Christ's sake, but you are prudent in Christ; we are weak, but you are strong; you are distinguished, but we are without honor. To this present hour we are both hungry and thirsty, and are poorly clothed, and are roughly treated, and are homeless; and we toil, working with our own hands; when we are reviled, we bless; when we are persecuted, we endure; when we are slandered, we try to conciliate; we have become as the scum of the world, the dregs of all things, even until now." 1Cor 4:9-13 (Emphasis Mine)

When we think of the Apostles of our Lord, we don't think of limousines, bodyguards, hotel rooms, or special privileges. Our minds will not likely gravitate toward kingship, alignment, dominion, or amassing great amounts of wealth. On the contrary, we picture these fishermen who walked the earth as servants of Christ, who gave their lives for the furtherance of the gospel. They did not see themselves as kings needing to be recognized, but merely as emissaries and bond slaves. They didn't brag about their anointing, or spheres of influence, or six sources of income, but only in the goodness and kindness of God. In the above passage, Paul, who was an educated scholar advanced above his contemporaries, was willing to go about homeless and poorly clothed to preach the gospel and serve the Church. These were humble men with great spiritual power, that laid the foundation of the Church. It is hard to imagine anyone with the audacity to suggest there is a new generation of apostles that can improve upon them or their ministry.

However, that is exactly what many in the NAR seem to be suggesting. In this chapter, I want to look at some claims and decrees of the movement that are Biblically unfounded, seriously lacking in humility, and promoting an elite class among believers.

Better Than the Early Church?

Just the very mention of a "New Apostolic Age" carries with it the idea that another is needed since the first one failed. But can there be two apostolic ages? The very concept itself is unbiblical. Jesus chose Twelve Apostles and sent them out to lay the foundation. Their ministry still exists today. Their teaching continues to be the foundation that all apostles are to build upon -- Christ Jesus Himself. Therefore, the emergence of apostles today is merely a return to the understanding, teaching and practice of the Twelve and the Church they established.

"All through the body of Christ there are many people who keep saying, 'Our church is not in very good shape now, and we need to get back to having a first-century church.' I couldn't disagree with that more. The last thing we need is a first-century church. What we need is a 21st-century church. We need a 21st-century church that's based on all the Biblical principles. Every time God has moved in the world through history-through the early church, through the Constantine time, through the Roman Empire, through the British colonization to our present day - He has always provided new wineskins. What we need to be tuned into is the new wineskins. The first-century church itself was a new wineskin; but now as we look back, it is one of the old wineskins. Jesus tells us that we should not return to the old wineskins because God is pouring out so much new wine."[11] (Emphasis Mine)

---

[11] *"The Church in the Marketplace,"* by C. Peter Wagner, *Regal Books*

I realize that our culture is different from that of the 1ˢᵗ Century Church; nevertheless, our practices and beliefs should not be. Honestly, to compare the Early Church with the Constantine period or the British Colonization is unimaginable. The above statement is coming from someone with different views on the end of the age than the Early Church. Have we really been given a "new wineskin?" The wineskin of the Early Church is old? Really? Wasn't that the wineskin given by Jesus? Isn't that the same as saying the structure of the New Testament Church has been replaced? If that's the case, then how do we know which principles to hold onto and which to discard? They may not have had cell phones or been able to put on conferences like the Church today, but we are not better than them. We may not wear the same kind of clothes, or live in the same kind of houses, but we have not been given a better "wineskin." On the contrary, the Holy Spirit is restoring our foundations and bringing us back to Biblical truth and practice. He is not giving us a "new paradigm" or a "new wineskin." Heaven forbid! Our responsibility is to imitate them as they imitated Christ and to do so in the culture we find ourselves in. This is the true apostolic reformation and revival work of the Holy Spirit!

"Since 2001, the body of Christ has been in the Second Apostolic Age. The apostolic/prophetic government of the church is now in place…. We began to build our base by locating and identifying with the intercessory prayer movements. This time, however, we feel that God wants us to start governmentally, connecting with the apostles of the region. God has already raised up for us a key apostle in one of the strategic nations of the Middle East, and other apostles are already coming on board. Once we have the apostles in place, we will then bring the intercessors and the prophets into the inner circle, and we will end up with the spiritual core we need

to move ahead for retaking the dominion that is rightfully ours."[12] (Emphasis Mine)

There is a lot of "we" and "us" in this passage. Last time I checked the dominion belonged to Him. Nowhere do the early apostles ever speak about taking dominion (more on this later) or bringing the intercessors and prophets into "the inner circle." What inner circle? With all due respect to the late Peter Wagner, this is not the language of humble servants of the Body of Christ.

"We have what we call the Seven Mountains mandate ...I'm commissioning you to become super wealthy. If you own the businesses of your country, you control what goes on in your country. You know what's going to happen. One day in our countries they're not going to say, 'Those Jews, you know they're so wealthy.' They're going to say, 'Oh you know those Christians, everything they do turns to gold, right? I mean, Look at that. They funded this university. Their name is on that hospital.' I have a dream. In the city of Dallas, one day there's going to be a group of entrepreneurs that work together. We're going to go the hospital and say, 'What's the most expensive piece of equipment you need and buy it. We're going to go to the symphony and say how much does it cost for a whole year of your programs and we're going to pay for it. We're going to go to the poorest schools and say what is your greatest need, probably computers or whatever, and we're going to do it. Until every single sector of society is funded by us, and we become the head and not the tail.... Listen the tail gets dragged around. Aren't you tired of being dragged around?"[13]

---

[12] C.P. Wagner, Global Link Newsletter Global Harvest Ministries, Dated: 1st November 2001
[13] Cindy Jacobs at a conference in Indonesia in 2008,
http://www.youtube.com/watch?v=tD6OmQe_t2U

Honestly, I believe that God will provide for His children out of His riches in glory, but these comments are arrogant, not to mention unflattering to Jews. Please consider the passage I opened the chapter with: *"For, I think, God has exhibited us apostles last of all...."* Is the gospel now about being rich philanthropists?

"I just had the privilege of meeting with the president of South Korea who is an apostle on the government mountain.... Then he became mayor of Seoul and when he became mayor of Seoul he dedicated the city to Jesus Christ and he got a lot of criticism by the Buddhists and he said, 'You know, this is my faith and I did what I did and I'm not going to take it back.' When you get to the top you can do some radical things for the Lord and unfortunately many of us are not at the top. And so, Deuteronomy 28:13 says we are to be the head and not the tail. If we share something concerning Christian values, we are persecuted because we are not at the head. Once we do get to the head, all of a sudden we can make decrees and declarations and we can influence that whole mountain"[14]

"This is the government of the Church of the future that will arise and spread My light throughout the world in the latter days. This government will overcome all other governments. When this is in order, you can then command the governments of the earth to come into order."[15]

This last quote is from the early days -- 2001. The government that is being spoken about is the NAR apostles. Once they are "in place," or "in order" then they can command the

---

[14] Interview with Che Ahn,
http://revivalfires.tv/ondemand/Che%20Ahn%20Who%20Are%20The%20Apostles.html
[15] *The Future War of the Church: How We Can Defeat Lawlessness and Bring God's Order to the Earth*, Chuck Pierce *Regal Books*, 2001, pages 31-32

governments of the earth to obey them. Does that sound like the attitude of the Apostles of our Lord? They certainly had apostles in place, and in order. So according to that logic, they should have commanded the Roman Empire to obey them. Instead, they told us to fix our hope completely on the revelation of Christ to come,[16] while in the meantime submitting ourselves to every human institution.[17] Not only did they have a different view of the Kingdom, they had a different attitude – one of humility.

Apostles First?

"And God has appointed in the church, first apostles, second prophets, third teachers, then miracles, then gifts of healings, helps, administrations, various kinds of tongues." 1Cor 12:28

CP Wagner comments on these verses in his book, *Apostles Today*:

"The numbers in the verse, proton (first), deuteron (second), and triton (third), indicate that this is not simply a random selection of gifts and offices. Proton in this instance should be interpreted to mean that apostles are first in order of sequence, not necessarily in importance of hierarchy. Hierarchy is an old-wineskin concept. To put it simply, a church without apostles will not function as well as a church with apostles."[18]

The above statement is good in that it acknowledges that the numbers contained in 1 Corinthians 12:28 are merely sequential and not hierarchical. With this I wholeheartedly agree. Incidentally, hierarchy is not just an old wineskin, it is a Dark

---

[16] 1 Peter 1:13
[17] 1 Peter 2:13
[18] Wagner, C. P. (2012-03-08). *Apostles Today* (p. 6). *Baker Publishing Group.*

Ages worldly structure that is thoroughly unbiblical. However, despite this admission concerning apostles being merely first in sequence here, the constant focus on the priority of the apostles, and the authority of the apostles, and submission to apostles, leads to the conclusion that apostles are pre-eminent. Indeed, there is such a preoccupation and veneration of apostles in the NAR, it would hardly be a surprise if they grew wings.

"Now that we are in the Second Apostolic Age, we recognize that pastors are not the spiritual gatekeepers of the city, as we once thought. Apostles, more specifically territorial apostles, must be seen as the spiritual gatekeepers of the city. Some of these territorial apostles will emerge from the nuclear Church and most likely will include certain megachurch pastors, but I am convinced that the great majority of them will come from the extended Church. Our workplace apostles have the greatest potential for leading the forces for city transformation. They are the ones most deeply embedded in the six non-church mountains, or molders, of culture. They are winners. They know how to make things happen once they are given the opportunity."[19]

To be in the NAR, one must learn a whole new language -- "Territorial apostles," and "nuclear church," and the "extended church." I assume the "nuclear church" is the one that meets on the corner of Smith and Main St, and the "extended church" is that Christian guy that has the business in the center of town. He has been to the church a few times and is convinced the pastor holds him back from being a mighty apostle. Perhaps you think I'm exaggerating here. I wish I was. But this kind of thing happens all the time. I have ministered to pastors who have

---

[19] C.P. Wagner, *Dominion! How Kingdom Action Can Change the World*, pp. 154-155

been disrespected, and even undermined, by so-called apostles without churches, because they were ordained or prophesied over by the NAR. And it's not surprising because this kind of teaching itself undermines pastors and local churches, who have also become secondary to the apostles.

Consider this from Bethel's Kris Vallotton in his book, *Heavy Rain: How to Flood Your World with God's Transforming Power*. After comparing pastors of local churches to the Pool of Bethesda and apostles to the river of Ezekiel, he has this to say:

"For the most part, the church has only empowered apostles to plant churches. But apostles were never meant merely to be church planters: they were called to be world changers. A leader can plant one hundred churches in cities around the world, but if those churches don't bring cultural transformation to their cities, then they are not apostolic. Cultural transformation is synonymous with apostolic ministry. Think about it. If we gather five thousand people week after week on a Sunday morning in a city of half a million, yet the crime rate remains unchanged, the cancer rate is unaffected, the divorce rate continues to grow, and the economy is in decline, what does that say about the people of God in that city?" [20]

This is heavy stuff! For a moment, I will try to put aside the unbelievable pressure and judgment coming from the rabid Dominion Theology of the passage, and just concentrate on my lack of apostolicity. If I am an apostle and not *just* a pastor, the crime rate and cancer rate and all other ills will be dropping in my city. I felt a bit sad when I decided to look up the statistics in Redding, CA, and saw that it was one of the top ten places in

---

[20] Kris Vallotton, *Heavy Rain: How to Flood Your World with God's Transforming Power*, by Chosen Books, 2016

the country where the crime rate was soaring.[21] A look at the cancer rate was equally depressing. Am I suggesting that Bethel and Kris Vallotton are wasting their time and are not doing an apostolic work? Absolutely not! Kris is doing that himself. It is his test for apostles. He and many like him in the Apostolic Dominion Movement are living in a Christian conference circuit bubble of unreality. They have convinced themselves they are changing the world when it is the Church they are changing, and not for the good. Nevertheless, there is more bad news coming for pastors and teachers.

"Pastorates are to some degree, irrelevant to their city's culture because their churches' governmental structures are built to congregate not to deploy…. Apostleships, on the other hand, are developed around the principle of training, equipping, and deploying the saints to radically alter society."[22]

How did pastors become irrelevant to their city's "culture?" We are about to find out. Something to do with supernatural flow! Another one of Bethel's Five-Folds puts it in a way we can understand. In a book that is ironically called, *Culture of Honor*, Danny Silk has this to say concerning 1 Corinthians 12:28:

"Paul clearly lays out an order of priority in this passage, and this order is related to the realms of the supernatural that correspond to each particular office…. When Paul makes apostles first, prophets second, and teachers third, he is describing a flow. The flow streams through the teacher, is released in miracles and healing, and continues through helps, and administrations and tongues. Tragically in many churches today, the practices of teaching, helps and administration have

---

[21] http://time.com/6729/10-cities-where-violent-crime-is-soaring/
[22] Kris Vallotton, *Heavy Rain: How to Flood Your World with God's Transforming Power*, by Chosen Books, 2016

become largely devoid of the supernatural. It seems as though these gifts were plucked out of the list and separated from the flow of the supernatural supply of heaven, and actually, that is exactly what has happened. In order to protect this flow, the church needs to be founded upon leaders who carry a primary core value for the supernatural.

Rather than having the apostle and prophet at the foundation of church culture, today the American church has largely placed the teacher, pastor, or evangelist at the helm. But effectively divorcing the supernatural from ministry in this way has drastically impacted the general understanding of the true role of each anointing.... The problem is that these are earthly focused models of leadership. Without the flow of grace from the apostles and prophets who are not only focused on seeing what is going on in heaven but also on releasing that reality here on earth, these models will inevitably lead us to focus on what we know God has done in the past and miss out on what He is doing now. They lead us to care more about knowledge than experience." [23]

Did you get that? There is a flow of the supernatural (heaven) that comes from the apostles and prophets through the teacher, helps, administration and tongues. The teachers and pastors, according to Silk, are earthly, inward, and selfish, and cannot have the supernatural in their lives without apostles. Apostles bring heaven down, and without their "river" flowing through them and their prophet sidekicks, the rest are doomed to live a life of dry, detached Christianity. Honestly, I find this teaching to be the most arrogant and dishonoring I have ever heard. And the way this book is being consumed by the Church worldwide is a grave sign for the outcome of the Apostolic Movement.

---

[23] Danny Silk, *Culture of Honor: Sustaining a Supernatural Environment*, Destiny Image Publishers, Pg. 45-47

For those of you who think I am taking his words out of some wonderful context, I can assure you I'm not. My wife and I were at the seminar live, and we lasted for little under an hour. It's all true, and apparently very entertaining for many who should know better. But there's more:

"The apostle will make the presence of God, the worship of God, and the agenda of Heaven the top priorities in the environment. An apostolic government is designed to protect these priorities."[24]

Talking about "levels of anointings" and speaking of the teacher he says:

"It's a C on the grade scale, and it's what keeps the church only average in its effects and influence."[25]

"When a pastoral anointing is the primary leader the people expect to be the center of the universe."[26]

If you have managed to pick yourself off the floor, then just sit down for a moment and let's consider what's wrong with this. For starters, whatever is flowing from the apostle here is not a teaching anointing. This is the most twisted and immature understanding of the Five-Fold Ministry imaginable, but it did not originate with Bethel's ministers. It is the standard exaltation of apostles and prophets that has been going on for years in the NAR. It is at best, seriously flawed, and at worst, dangerously arrogant. The purpose of all the Five-Fold Ministers is to serve the body of Christ and not exalt themselves. All of God's people

---

[24] Ibid, pg. 50
[25] Ibid pg. 54
[26] Danny Silk, *Culture of Honor: Sustaining a Supernatural Environment*, Destiny Image Publishers, Pg.71

are to be spiritual and filled with the Spirit. The flow of life comes from Jesus and not the apostles. He is the vine and we are the branches. Apostles are not the only ones who can "see what's going on in heaven." Neither are they above pastors or teachers. They need pastoring as much as anybody and they certainly need to be filled with the Word. In fact, how can there be such a thing as an apostle who is not a teacher, and is not able to accurately handle the Word of God? Where do we see that in Scripture? The Apostles in the New Testament saw into heaven more than any of these folks, yet they devoted themselves to prayer and the ministry of the Word.[27] Sadly, this is the very reason that the Revival Movement is rife with dangerous heresies after only twenty years, because its leaders, the "apostles," have always had a disdain for teaching and real Biblical scholarship.

The number system in 1 Corinthians 12:28 is not intended as some sort of grading levels of spirituality. If this were the case, pastors would be under people with the helps ministry, and just a little bit more important than tongues. This is nonsensical and obviously not what's being said. It is not about an order of ministries. If it were, only ministries would be mentioned and not gifts. And evangelists or pastors would not have been left out. Likewise, it is not about an order of gifts or only gifts would have been mentioned, and it would say prophecy and not prophets. Why then does Paul give this list?

What seems to be missing from the discussion of 1 Corinthians 12:28 is usually the context. Remember, Paul is admonishing the Corinthians concerning order in spiritual gifts and ministries. In chapters 1 through 4, he was addressing their immaturity concerning different ministries. Do you recall the conclusion? --

---

[27] Acts 6:4

"I planted and Apollos watered." Then in chapter 12, he is discussing the function of gifts.

"Now there are varieties of gifts, but the same Spirit. And there are varieties of ministries, and the same Lord." 1 Cor 12:4-5

This is the backdrop for verse 28. It explains why he includes ministries and gifts in the same sequence. Remember how big an issue they were having with tongues in Corinth? This is probably why it is last on the list. Nevertheless, when one considers the contents of the list, they are all necessary to plant the Church, grow it, and empower it to make disciples. I believe that is the point being made -- that the gifts and ministries have a purpose and strategy. Putting it simply, apostles (the ones sent) preach the gospel and lay the foundation, which is Christ. Prophets confirm and strengthen the believers in their relationship with God, and teachers help them to become grounded in the Word. Consider what Paul and Barnabas did in Antioch, teaching for a whole year (teaching was a huge part of the ministry of the Early Church). Then miracles and gifts of healing function in a way to minister to the Church, but also to evangelize. Helps are essential to get things done, especially today, since churches need property and the set-up of chairs and equipment, etc. Then the administration of the Church is put in place with elders being appointed. This was usually done prior to the apostolic team leaving. Then tongues are mentioned as an ongoing part of Church life. Thus, the Church is planted and grows and the process begins all over again. So, the apostolic is first and the Church itself must be apostolic in its vision and focus. But in no way do these ministries operate independent of each other. Also, in the Early Church we can see that most of the teaching was done by the Apostles themselves, who were obviously teachers. Perhaps many would consider this too simple an explanation. But it is the business of teachers to try and make complicated things simple, and this is what Paul was attempting to do.

The Use of Titles

"They love the place of honor at banquets and the chief seats in the synagogues, and respectful greetings in the market places, and being called Rabbi by men. But do not be called Rabbi; for One is your Teacher, and you are all brothers. Do not call anyone on earth your father; for One is your Father, He who is in heaven. Do not be called leaders; for One is your Leader, that is, Christ. But the greatest among you shall be your servant. Whoever exalts himself shall be humbled; and whoever humbles himself shall be exalted." Mt 23:8-12

A pastor friend of mine was telling me how he had been approached by a group of these apostles. When they introduced themselves, they said, this is "Apostle John," and this is "Apostle Tom" and the one over here is "Apostle Terry." He looked at me with a sad look and said, "We thought they were just kidding, but we found out later, they were serious."

The use of titles for Christian leaders has always been a problem in the Church. However, with the emergence of the NAR it has now become fashionable and honorable and even braggadocios. Many in the NAR advocate the use of titles and, despite the words of Jesus, they try to say it is Biblical. Some even see it as their duty to use titles. Though there is not total agreement in the movement, the consensus seems to be that it is a good thing. Consider this from Dr. Dan Cheatham:

"Never refer to your spiritual father by first name alone in the presence of others. At least call him, 'Pastor Bob' or 'Bishop' or 'Brother Thompson' or 'Dr. Smith.' Uphold God's authority that

He has delegated to men. Uphold spiritual authority because one day your own authority in the Lord will need to be upheld. See yourself as a pillar upholding the authority and anointing of God in the midst of His church."[28]

This is surely an appalling use of titles, but it is very common today and I believe it says something about spiritual pride and ego. I have never been comfortable with the term "pastor" being used as a first name, and once people know me, they usually won't do that anymore. However, now folks are dropping the term pastor in favor of being called "Apostle So and So." This is happening even in churches that are not aligned with the NAR. Furthermore, there is a lifestyle that goes with this mentality. The "Apostle" is treated like a rock star who comes into the service half-way through the worship, and gets ushered in and out. This kind of behavior is clearly in disobedience to the words of Jesus. He said we were not to be called Rabbi, Teacher, Father or even Leader. Many argue that Paul and the Apostles used titles, but this is absolutely false. They referred to themselves as apostles and bond slaves, but always as a function and not a title. For instance, Paul often introduced himself as "Paul, an apostle (or emissary) of Jesus Christ." All the others did the same. No one ever used a title instead of a name. This is quite different and not acceptable to the Lord. This one is a no-brainer. And there is no excuse for culture. When ministers insist on being called by titles, it is either that they have not heard what Jesus said, or an indication of spiritual pride and disobedience. It is not the heart of a servant. On the contrary, it elevates leaders above the congregation and contributes to a clergy-laity class system. There is no problem with the title if it comes after your name. This does not in any way suggest that pastors and leaders should not be honored. Indeed, they should

---

[28] *Apostolic Alignment: Finding Our Place* by Dr. Dan Cheatham

be honored by the congregation for their work and service. Nevertheless, there is no excuse for disobeying the words of the Lord. I have found that those who are truly functioning as apostles are generally those who have been broken of pride and are quite happy to be loved and viewed as parents rather than celebrities. They are those who want the glory to go to Him alone!

Angels Reassigned?

As an addendum to this section, I just want to add one more fascinating piece of breaking news regarding NAR apostles. We have heard already how they bring heaven down, and how they are the river flowing and all that! But now we are told that the angels are abandoning the denominational leaders altogether, in favor of the New Apostles.

"It is my personal conviction that one of the essential elements that has ushered in this apostolic age is that the angels no longer recognize the performance-based authority of denominationalism. Paul teaches us that angels recognize true spiritual authority. In fact, it is the angels who answer our prayers and fulfill our prophecies (see 1 Corinthians 11:4, 10). Angels are mentioned more than 180 times in the New Testament alone. Where have all the angels gone in the twenty-first-century Church? What would the world be like if we were suddenly to employ angelic help on this planet in the same degree as they did in the first century? I think that as we are reformed into this new apostolic wineskin, we are about to find out."[29]

This statement seems over-the-top arrogant, even for the NAR. Nevertheless, there it is. Did you know this? Does your dear Assemblies of God pastor know that the angels won't work with

---

[29] *Where Have All the Angels Gone*, Kris Vallotton, *Charisma Magazine*, 9/13/2016

him anymore, since he belongs to a denomination? What a shocker! I can tell you this comment sends shivers up my spine. I suppose this also applies to local "non-aligned" churches. With the angels only working with NAR apostles, this means, I suppose, they are the only ones authorized by heaven? Therefore, if you don't line up with them, angels will no longer recognize you or help you. Can you feel the love of the Father in this? This is like something one would expect to hear from a bishop or cardinal during the darkest days of the church!

Conclusion

When it comes to the subject of apostles being first, in the sense that they are over the other ministers authoritatively, there is no support for this in Scripture. All the ministries were honored, and those that were true to the faith gave themselves to spreading the gospel and teaching and shepherding the flock that Christ purchased with His own blood. These precious people lived their lives as bondservants, caring for and serving God's people. Though they had great stature because of their Christlikeness, and great confidence because of His calling and choosing them, they never saw themselves as superior to other genuine ministers. We have their lives and the Scriptures as proof. Peter, who was a leader among the Twelve, and close to the Lord, referred to himself as a fellow elder, or "co-leader" in our vernacular. What then, is all the talk about needing a "new wineskin?" What's wrong with the example they gave? What more do we need?

It seems clear that those in the New Apostolic Reformation have begun to idolize apostles and prophets. They seem to fancy themselves very highly and speak of apostles not as the scum of the earth, but as the saviors of the Church and the world. The Bible warns us that those who exalt themselves will be humbled, and that pride goes before destruction. It is my firm conviction that, despite the good things in the movement and the valid aspects of restoration, this whole experiment has become a massive head trip -- a huge ego balloon that will one day burst. Then will come crying, sorrow and pain, when reality sets in and they realize they have spent their lives chasing structure instead of Christ. Dear friend, if you are an apostle, or a prophet, stay true to Jesus and His Word and just do the work. Remember, when it's all said and done, much more is said than done. When you stand before the Lord, He won't be calling you an apostle, but a servant. He will either say, "Well done, good and faithful servant," or "Depart from me you who practice lawlessness."

Chapter Three
Defining an Apostle
(The Biblical Five-Fold)

"A Christian leader who is gifted, taught, and commissioned by God with the authority to establish the foundational government of the Church within an assigned sphere of ministry by hearing what the Spirit is saying to the churches and by setting things in order accordingly for the advancement of the Kingdom of God."[30]

The above definition is quite commonly used by the various apostolic movements, although they admit it is not complete. Nevertheless, most will emphasize government and foundations in the ministry of an apostle and some go as far as to say that apostles themselves are the foundation of the Church. Though there is much that is true in these definitions, they also contain presuppositions which are inaccurate and can be misleading. When definitions such as these are taken as authoritative, they replace the Biblical understanding should it be different. Indeed, if we accept this definition of an apostle as one who "hears what the Spirit is saying to the churches and sets things in order accordingly," then it seems all we must do is hear what the "apostle" is saying to the Church and align with it, which is of course what many are doing. Consequently, the Biblical admonition to hear what the Spirit is saying, or what the Word has said, is replaced in the minds of the followers of these movements. However, compare this conclusion with the words of Paul when he said to the Galatians that if any man or even an angel from heaven were to preach a different gospel other that the one he had preached, he should be accursed.[31] Obviously,

---

[30] Attributed to C. Peter Wagner and posted on the ICA website
http://www.coalitionofapostles.com/about-ica/definition-of-apostle
[31] Gal 1:8-9

Paul was not suggesting that we disregard our leaders, since he himself had submitted his understanding of the gospel to the Apostles at Jerusalem.[32] Instead, he was reaffirming in no uncertain terms, that there is one gospel and one truth given by the Lord and His Apostles that we must hold onto, discarding anything that would contradict. Thus, all Christians should know that any "present truth" which is coming by revelation, needs to be aligned with Scripture in word and principle or it is to be rejected, regardless of who has spoken it, or who has accepted it. I will come back to this theme later but I trust I have illustrated the problem with extra-Biblical definitions. This is not to say that the author of this definition meant for it to be received this way but it will be regardless, because as it is written, it is flawed. Let us proceed then to examine the Biblical usage of the term apostle and see how the current teaching lines up with it.

The term "apostle" comes from the Greek word *apostolos* meaning "one sent forth from another" (apo - from, stello - to send). Thus, a simple definition of an apostle is one who has been sent as a messenger, or a delegate, or an emissary from another with a mission or message. It is understood that the emissary has the authority of the sender and represents the sender. Jesus chose twelve disciples whom He designated Apostles, and sent them out with a message and with His authority. They uniquely represent Him[33] throughout this age and the next. Though the Lord sent out many other apostles, the most notable being Paul, and continues to send out apostles, the Twelve are unique in their calling and choosing. However, the idea of an apostle is not unique to the New Testament, hence the lack of explanation by Jesus or others. In fact, this is true of all New Testament leadership which is merely a continuation of what was already understood by the Jews. The

[32] Gal 2:2
[33] Mt 19:28, Acts 1:15-26, Rev 21:14

equivalent of *apostolos* in the Hebrew Scriptures is probably *malach,* meaning a deputy or messenger, and in the Septuagint, *aggelos* (pronounced "angelos") also for messenger or angel. The Hebrew verb *shalach* (to send) is used in relation to the sending of Moses and others such as Elijah, Jeremiah and Ezekiel. This is the origin of the Hebrew term *shaliach* which continues to be used by religious Jews today, although since Biblical times it has taken on more of a legal meaning. The *shaliach* (emissary) would also be an equivalent to the apostle. This is confirmed by the translation of the word *shalach* (to send) as *apostello* in the Septuagint.[34] Also, the author of Hebrews refers to Jesus as an apostle over His house and likens Him to Moses who was also faithful over his house, and presumably also an apostle. Thus, we see clearly that the New Testament writers did not view an apostle as some new "office" that had been created by Jesus but merely a continuation of an old custom of sending emissaries. Jesus, in His denunciation of His generation, said this:

"For this reason also the wisdom of God said, 'I will send to them prophets and apostles, and some of them they will kill and some they will persecute, in order that the blood of all the prophets, shed since the foundation of the world, may be charged against this generation...." Luke 11:49-50 (Emphasis Mine)

Here Jesus is saying that He will send apostles and prophets before the destruction of Jerusalem when all the blood of the slain prophets was charged against that generation. Now we know He chose Twelve Apostles and later the Holy Spirit released others, but where does it say He chose prophets? This is where Greek thinking breaks down. Westerners are essentially Greek thinkers. The Greeks wanted logic. Westerners like to

---

[34] LXX (Brenton) 2Chron: 36:15

have all their ducks in a row and everything neatly labeled. In our culture, we label everything that we don't understand and then proclaim that we understand it. The ancient Hebrews were much more emotive and tended to communicate that way. Thus, we often find that their thoughts and terms overlap and are rarely defined since they were understood culturally and not just linguistically. They not only spoke a different language, they looked at the world differently. And since they wrote the Bible we need to understand their perspective to understand their terms. Jesus did not choose twelve prophets and send them out, but He did choose twelve disciples as His special emissaries. Luke tells us He named them "apostles" but we know that Jesus was not speaking in Greek, therefore, what Hebrew or Aramaic term did He use? Also, were not some or all of them prophets? Who would dare say the Apostle John was not a prophet? Indeed, the whole "Five-Fold Ministry"[35] may have been represented by one or all of them, but they were not called apostles until they were sent. Then, as if to frustrate our Greek minds, Matthew records Jesus' words differently.

"Therefore, behold I am sending you prophets and wise men and scribes; some of them you will kill and crucify, and some of them you will scourge in your synagogues, and persecute from city to city…" Mt 23:34 (Emphasis Mine)

This verse speaks about the same people that Jesus sent, yet there is no mention of apostles. Instead we are told they are prophets, wise men (watchmen) and scribes (scholars). The clear implication is that the apostles were prophets, wise men and scholars. They may not have begun this way, but they entered into it. Either that or Jesus is saying that He sent some prophets, some watchmen, and some scholars. Whatever way you slice it,

---

[35] This term is applied to the five ministries listed in Eph 4:11, but is not in itself a Biblical term.

they were apostles because He sent them to represent Him. Scholars, of course, are seasoned teachers -- a rare breed today. And the thought of a teacher being an apostle would send shivers up the spine of the NAR since by their reckoning, teachers are not apostles and less important in the "Five-Fold Ministry." But if that is so, then Jesus surely should have known it and been clearer and not opened the door for teachers and watchmen to be considered apostles. Some would argue that Jesus was being very general, whereas the Apostles, especially Paul, cleared things up later and gave definition to the various ministries. There is no question that Paul did give us some further insight, but is there any indication he viewed things differently? Let us consider for a moment his sending out from Antioch to see if there is anything further we can learn about apostles.

The Apostolic Church of Antioch

The church in Antioch is considered the model church as far as today's apostles are concerned. Presumably because they were apostolic, sending out Paul and Barnabas, and they didn't have the "religious spirit" problems which seem to be associated with Jerusalem. This thinking is typical, yet it is brought on by an anti-Jewish bias that has no basis in truth. The fact that the church at Antioch was not considered the model is clear by the actions of its leaders. Though it was indeed a good church, and certainly a model, its leaders clearly looked to Jerusalem for guidance and covering, as did all the churches -- and for good reason: The Apostles of our Lord were residing there. When an issue arose in Antioch concerning the Judaizers, they sent Paul and Barnabas to Jerusalem to the Apostles and elders to sort the matter out and bring order, something which they could not do.[36] Furthermore, Paul himself told the Galatians that he went

---

[36] Acts 15

46

to Jerusalem to the Apostles to check out his own doctrine to be sure it was consistent with theirs,[37] even though he was emphatic that he had not received his commissioning from men but from the Lord Himself. By this act he demonstrated not only his humility, but his reverence and submission to the message given to the Twelve and the Jerusalem congregation. Also, much later in his ministry he came to the church in Jerusalem and once again submitted himself to the elders without debate, realizing that they were wisely trying to protect the integrity of his ministry.[38] Thus the idea that the Antioch church was the apostolic church instead of Jerusalem, which continues to be taught today, is a fallacy clearly intended to undermine the Twelve and their work in favor of Paul, who is practically regarded as a Gentile.

The teaching on apostles that is dominating the Church today gives the impression that apostles are very different in gifting and makeup than the other ministries. We hear much about the "office" of the apostle and how it is primary and greater. Yet, as we shall see, when we put the body of Scripture on the subject together, it is difficult to conclude that an apostle has a different gifting than that of the others. This is clearly borne out in the sending of Paul and Barnabas mentioned in Acts 13.

"Now there were at Antioch, in the church that was there, prophets and teachers: Barnabas, and Simeon who was called Niger, and Lucius of Cyrene, and Manaen who had been brought up with Herod the tetrarch, and Saul. While they were ministering to the Lord and fasting, the Holy Spirit said, 'Set apart for Me Barnabas and Saul for the work to which I have called them.' Then, when they had fasted and prayed and laid their hands on them, they sent them away. So, being sent out

---

[37] Gal 2:2
[38] Acts 21:19-26

by the Holy Spirit, they went down to Seleucia and from there they sailed to Cyprus." Acts 13:1-4 (Emphasis Mine)

This passage starts off by saying that at Antioch there were prophets and teachers. This is a fascinating statement which raises many questions yet it is usually overlooked in discussions of apostolic ministry. Why prophets and teachers? Were there no pastors or evangelists? And where are the apostles? What? The great apostolic center has no apostles? How can this be? Surely Paul was an apostle since the Lord had called and chosen him personally many years before? Yet Luke, who is aware of this, does not refer to Paul as an apostle until after the sending. This could be because Paul, who undoubtedly told the story to Luke, did not see himself this way until after the Holy Spirit had set him apart at Antioch. From then on both men are referred to by Luke as apostles,[39] since they were sent out as emissaries of Christ by the Holy Spirit to preach the gospel and establish churches in every city. This is the work to which the Holy Spirit called them and sent them.

Another fact that is usually unnoticed in this account is that Paul and Barnabas were either prophets or teachers. When it says, "there were prophets and teachers," it does not differentiate which they were. Paul was certainly a teacher[40] and a prophet as we clearly see later.[41] And who can say he wasn't an evangelist or a shepherd (pastor)? Yet on this occasion, before his traveling ministry began, he is referred to as either a prophet or a teacher. It is likely that he and Barnabas are both seen as teachers, since Luke tells us they had been teaching the church for an entire year prior to this event.[42] In either case, the point is

---

[39] Acts 14:14
[40] 1 Tim 2:7, 2 Tim 1:11
[41] 2Cor 12:7
[42] Acts 11:25

clearly established that teachers and prophets can be called as apostles by the Holy Spirit and sent out to preach the gospel and plant churches and lay foundations. So much for the idea being circulated today by the NAR that teachers sow division because of their concern about doctrine, and apostles instead bring unity. Obviously, this is another fallacy since teachers can also be apostles!

The Foundation of Apostles

"So then you are no longer strangers and aliens, but you are fellow citizens with the saints, and are of God's household, having been built on the foundation of the apostles and prophets, Christ Jesus Himself being the corner stone, in whom the whole building, being fitted together, is growing into a holy temple in the Lord, in whom you also are being built together into a dwelling of God in the Spirit." Eph 2:19-20 (Emphasis Mine)

From this passage, many are boldly proclaiming that apostles and prophets are the foundation of the Church. Indeed, as far as the Charismatic and Revival Movements are concerned, this is an indisputable fact. Some do point out that apostles and prophets are not themselves the foundation, but they often go on to make them the foundation anyway. Yet, this passage does not say that apostles and prophets are the foundation of the Church. It clearly states that the Church is built on the foundation of *the* Apostles and Prophets. The article in the Greek cannot be omitted. It is "*the* Apostles" and "*the* Prophets," and not just any apostle or prophet. "*The* Apostles" are the Twelve Apostles of the Lamb and "*the* Prophets" are the Prophets of Israel.[43] No First-Century Jew would have seen it any

---

[43] 2 Pet 3:2

other way and this is clearly what the text says. Furthermore, it is not the Apostles and Prophets themselves, but the foundation that was laid by them, which of course is the revelation of the Messiah, Christ Jesus Himself -- the Cornerstone. The Prophets of Israel spoke of the Messiah and His Kingdom and the Apostles used their words, as well as their own personal knowledge, to reveal Him. Paul is telling the Gentile believers that they have been brought into the household of God and have also been built on this foundation. The Early Church was committed to *the* Apostles' teaching[44] which was about Christ and not just "apostolic teaching," which today could be about anything. Jesus alone is the foundation of the Church and not ministers of any kind. This was made very clear by Jesus when He told Peter that the Church would be built upon the revelation that he had received of the Messiah,[45] and by Paul who declared that no other foundation can be laid other than the one he laid which was Christ Himself.[46] Thus, even if one were to argue concerning the use of the article in Ephesians 2, the foundation would still be Christ and the revelation of Him.

"Equipping the saints is one thing, but some will say that it is not necessarily governing. True, so let's go back a couple of chapters to Ephesians 2:20, where Paul describes the church as the 'household of God.' He explains that the church is 'built on the foundation of the apostles and prophets, Jesus Christ Himself being the chief cornerstone (vs 20).' In a broad theological sense, Jesus is, of course, the foundation of the church because, as I have discussed, He came to earth in order to institute it. However, according to this Scripture, after He ascended and sent the Holy Spirit, He left the nuts and bolts of building the church to the leadership of apostles and prophets.

---

[44] Acts 2:42
[45] Mt 16:16-20
[46] 1Cor 3:11-12

Jesus is still there, but as the cornerstone, not as the foundation itself. The cornerstone holds the foundation together, but the foundation itself is clearly apostles and prophets."[47]

In this rendition of Ephesians 2:20, Jesus is pushed to the side as the foundation in a "broad theological sense," but not as the functional foundation, or the "nuts and bolts" foundation. In other words, He is sort of a ceremonial foundation, a figurehead, while the real foundation is the new apostles and prophets themselves. Also, He is the Cornerstone, but one that appears to have more of a ceremonial role like the cornerstones of today.

There is perhaps no statement more disturbing, or more offensive in all the NAR teaching, than this. It truly is the foundation upon which they have built -- themselves! They have replaced Jesus with themselves, and their ministries. This is the focus of their writings and all their activity. What a disaster, and the fruit of it is a Church that is massively confused about everything, especially its future and identity. However, Jesus is the foundation, which, of course, is the point being made in Ephesians 2:20. It is Him, He is the foundation, the Cornerstone, and the whole building is not only built on Him, it is to be built up in Him in all aspects. Furthermore, Jesus is the builder, who said, "I will build My Church." The Five-Fold Ministry is supposed to build up the Church, teaching and ministering to it under the direct guidance and leadership of Christ. He is the foundation and functional head of the Church and not a figurehead.

It would, of course, be valid to say that based on Ephesians 2:20, apostles and prophets are ministries that lay the foundation (Jesus) in the lives of believers. Yet, surely the same must be true

---

[47] *The Church in the Workplace: How God's People Can Transform Society*, by C. Peter Wagner, pg., 23

for evangelists, pastors and teachers. Indeed, all our preaching and teaching should be laying this foundation and building on it with more of the same. Otherwise, according to Paul, we are building with wood, hay, and straw -- things destined to be burned up.[48] Christ is not just the foundation, He is the whole building, and we must be careful not to build anything in the believers that does not bring more devotion to Him.[49] Knowing Him more, and loving Him more and longing for His appearing, is the true apostolic message since it is the message of the Apostles.[50] Therefore, any teaching that is producing another focus or preoccupation in believers or movements is not genuinely apostolic.

Another passage that seems to single out apostles and prophets is the following:

"By referring to this, when you read you can understand my insight into the mystery of Christ, which in other generations was not made known to the sons of men, as it has now been revealed to His holy apostles and prophets in the Spirit; to be specific, that the Gentiles are fellow heirs and fellow members of the body, and fellow partakers of the promise in Christ Jesus through the gospel..." Eph 3:4-6 (Emphasis Mine)

The context here is the revelation of the mystery that God had made the Gentile believers fellow heirs with the Jewish believers, which of course is the context of the previous passage as well. Paul says that this mystery, which was hidden to the previous generations, was now revealed to His holy apostles and prophets in or by the Spirit. Paul does not use the article here as in the previous passage. He does not say that it has now been

---

[48] 1Cor 3:10-16
[49] 2Cor 11:3
[50] Eph 1:17, Col 1:10, 2:2, 3:10,2Tim 4:8, 2Pet 1:3, 3:18

revealed to *the* Apostles and Prophets but rather His holy apostles and prophets. Undoubtedly, that includes the Twelve, but also others, since Paul himself is obviously included. The use of the term "prophets" here may or may not be referencing individuals other than the Apostles, since they clearly brought the revelation from God and would be considered prophets. They were prophets and emissaries. Paul may in fact be referring to the council in Jerusalem when the Apostles and elders, himself included, came to this conclusion. In any event, it does not suggest that apostles and prophets are some special class and that teachers, pastors and evangelists are not in this company. Such thinking is distinctly Western, inflexible, and out of step with the facts of Scripture. For instance, Philip was an evangelist and most likely a prophet. I make that deduction from the fact that he had four virgin daughters who were prophetesses. You must agree that something very prophetic was going on in that household. Also, judging from his incredible ministry with signs and wonders in Samaria, and his transportation by the Spirit to Azotus, we can conclude that he was very strong in the revelatory gifts. Consequently, it would seem that evangelists can be prophets. And why not? Can't evangelists speak for God? Today Philip would probably be called a "prophetic evangelist" or an "evangelistic prophet." Regardless, there is a significant case to be made for the overlapping of the so-called "Five-Fold."

The Five-Fold Ministry

"But to each one of us grace was given according to the measure of Christ's gift. Therefore it says, 'When He ascended on high, He led captive a host of captives, And He gave gifts to men.' (Now this expression, 'He ascended,' what does it mean except that He also had descended into the lower parts of the earth? He who descended is Himself also He who ascended far

above all the heavens, so that He might fill all things.) And He gave some as apostles, and some as prophets, and some as evangelists, and some as pastors and teachers, for the equipping of the saints for the work of service, to the building up of the body of Christ; until we all attain to the unity of the faith, and of the knowledge of the Son of God, to a mature man, to the measure of the stature which belongs to the fullness of Christ." Ephesians 4:7-13 (Emphasis Mine)

The above passage is the proof text for the Five-Fold Ministry teaching common in the Church. I personally believe in the existence and restoration of these functions today, and spent nearly twenty years in a movement of churches that majored in this passage, and the restoration of apostles and prophets. Nevertheless, I believe that conclusions have been drawn from here to advance certain agendas that are out of step with the intentions of Paul and the Holy Spirit who inspired him. For this reason, I would like to invite you to take another look at the passage, putting aside what you have been taught, to see if the common conclusions are altogether legitimate.

The first thing we must be careful to do is not take verse 11 out of its context and make it the focal point. The context of the passage can clearly be seen by the verses before and after. The Five-Fold Ministry is not the focus; rather it is the fullness of Christ and the maturing of the Body in this fullness, love and unity. The high holy calling of the Church is the clear message to the Ephesians, and the mention of the various giftings of leaders is not intended as a thorough explanation, but only a passing reference, albeit accurate. He begins the brief mention of leadership with verse 7, reminding everyone that we have each received a different measure of grace or gifting in the Messiah. He backs that up with a passage from the Psalms,[51] and

---

[51] Ps 68:18

goes on to explain that these different graces or ministries were given to equip and mature the Body into the fullness of Christ and unity in *the* faith, by speaking the truth in love. He contrasts that with false teachers and ministries that are causing the saints to be carried about by waves of doctrine and by trickery, craftiness, and deceitful scheming. This is the point of the reference to church leadership in the passage. He then goes on to give practical instruction on holy living and staying filled up with the Holy Spirit and power.[52] So we must be careful not to make too much about the ministers mentioned instead of the results of their ministry, which is the whole point. True godly ministers make a fuss about Christ rather than themselves, and they bring the Body into truth and maturity rather than bouncing them around from one crafty teaching to another, designed to make themselves the focus. The Church would do well to concentrate on the truth and consequences of the messages being preached rather than aligning with apostolic celebrities.

The second question to consider is the so-called "Ascension Gift Ministries" themselves. Did Jesus give gifts or ministries? Are they gifts or callings? Some suggest that the people themselves are the gifts and not just the giftings that they possess. They get this by putting the statement that "He gave gifts to men" with "and He gave some as apostles," etc. Thus, they conclude that there is a "gift" of an apostle. While it is certainly true that apostles themselves are gifts to the Church, as are all genuine ministries, is there such a thing as a gift of "apostle?" If there is, then only apostles can have it, and all the other Five-Fold Ministries cannot. Therefore, they cannot be apostles. Yet, we have already seen that they were in Scripture.[53]

---

[52] Eph 5:18-19, 6:10
[53] Acts 13:1-4

Another point can be made that when we look at the nine gifts of the Spirit listed in 1Corinthians 12, or the seven giftings listed in Romans 12, we do not see the gift of apostle or the gift of pastor or even the gift of evangelist mentioned. We do see the gift of prophecy and the gift of teaching and the gift of leadership, but none of the others are mentioned as gifts. Why? Could it be that in Ephesians 4:11, Paul is simply listing the five different functions of leadership in the Church rather than five different leadership gifts? I realize that many will say Paul listed apostles as the foremost among gifts in 1Corinthians 12:20, but an equally strong case can be made that he listed both functions and gifts in a certain order, since apostles are people and miracles are not. In other words, why start off with apostles and prophets and teachers and then change to miracles, gifts of healings, helps, administrations and tongues? These are not people or ministries, but gifts. So, is it a list of gifts or a list of ministries or both? I believe it is both, in a certain order, and for a certain purpose. The "apostles" use this verse to point out that they are first and most important among the ministries; however, they never deal with the rest of the verse. And pastors and evangelists never use it since they are not mentioned at all. So what is the conclusion? Is there an apostle gift? The answer is no. Apostleship is not a gift but a calling. Paul makes this clear in his introduction to Romans and 1 Corinthians when he says he is "a called apostle."[54] Though he was affirmed by the church at Antioch, he makes it clear in Galatians that he was called by God and not the agency of man.[55] What happened in Antioch is that the Holy Spirit re-commissioned Paul, making it clear to the Church and gave him Barnabas as a companion, who from that time on was also called an apostle.[56] Thus apostles are called and commissioned by God the Holy Spirit. That's what makes

---

[54] Rom 1:1, 1Cor 1:1
[55] Gal 1:1
[56] Acts 14:14

them apostles. What is also clear is that they did not begin their ministries as apostles, except in the case of the Twelve, but as either teachers or prophets and were functioning in that "Five-Fold" capacity before they became apostles.

Born Five-Fold?

While we are born with natural gifts and even personalities that aid us in our ministry calling, no one is born an apostle or prophet. Indeed, we are not even born Christians. We must become believers and be filled with the Spirit before that process can begin. The only apostles and prophets born as such were John the Baptist, and Jesus the Messiah. And even they had to grow up and be taught. My knowledge of Scripture tells me that everyone else was called and commissioned by the Lord and sent out later in life. It seems almost silly to have to point this out, yet when you hear these apostles speaking today, you would think that they just came floating down from heaven as apostolic gifts to the world.

Another reality is that apostles, if they did not have one or more of the other giftings, would not be apostles since there would be little accomplished by sending them. Thus, apostles are those that are sent out as emissaries or ambassadors or whatever you like, but there is not a gift of apostle.

Another point that needs to be made from Ephesians 4:11 is regarding the very structure of the verse itself in the Greek. The conjunction *men de* means, "on the one hand and on the other hand." It suggests a contrast though most Greek scholars say it is mild. But it is a contrast nonetheless. Most of our translations say *"he gave some as apostles, some as prophets,"* etc. But what the Greek actually says is: *"He gave some on the one hand, the apostles and on the other hand the prophets, the evangelists, the shepherds and teachers."* It appears the scholars all felt it was necessary to leave it out to make the passage more understandable, since in their minds it was not significant. But why? And what if they are wrong? What if there is a bias coming through from the translators that once eliminated, may make the passage more understandable. Though the scholars of Bible translations usually are and were dedicated to accuracy, biases still occur. For instance, in the same passage the word *poimen* is translated "pastor," whereas everywhere else it occurs in the New Testament it is translated "shepherd." Yet no reason is ever given for this change. Also, in a discussion about the administration of a special collection from the churches, Paul refers to the brothers with him, other than Titus, as "apostles." The word is clearly *apostoloi* which should be translated "apostles" and not *aggelos* which would be translated "messengers."[57] Yet in all the translations, without exception, it is translated "messengers." What is the reason for this decision? Why "messengers" here and "apostles" everywhere else? Obviously, the translators seem to feel that such a task as this would be demeaning to the title "apostle," and more suited to the title "messenger." Could this same bias also exist in the translation of Ephesians 4:11? Why did Paul put the contrast there in verse 11? Why not simply say what the translators have translated, which says, Christ gave five different ministries instead of "on the one hand apostles" and "on the other" the other four? Why the distinction? Could it be that Paul is contrasting apostles since they are taken from the other ministries and are not necessarily a separate ministry? In other words, from the list of four ministry functions that operate in local churches, some are selected by the Holy Spirit and sent as emissaries to the universal Body of Believers, in the same way as Paul and Barnabas. So, what then can we conclude regarding

---

[57] 2Cor 8:23

the definition of an apostle? Before we get to that, let's look at some more anomalies in relation to the Five-Fold Ministry.

Five-Fold Overlap

When leaders in the church today speak of the Five-Fold Ministries they almost always present a picture of five totally distinct giftings or callings. Though there are five mentioned in Ephesians 4:11, and all exist in the Church today, there is no neatly labeled operation of these ministries either in Scripture or Church experience. Paul was an apostle to the Church, yet he clearly functioned as a teacher, a prophet, an evangelist, and a shepherd. Indeed, he is still operating in these ministries today, through the pages of the Bible, as are the other apostles and New Testament writers. The five ministries represent the ministry of Christ to the Church. Five is the number of service and their service is intended to bring the Church to maturity in the faith. Someone once compared the Five-Fold Ministry to the hand of Christ with five fingers. It is a good analogy which captures the essence of what ministry is all about; namely, service. It suggests that apostles are the thumb which can touch all the other fingers and which is essential to their proper working (some would argue that the thumb is not a finger). The index finger is likened to the prophet, the middle and longest finger to the evangelist, the ring finger to the pastor and the pinky to the teacher who gives balance. It's all good and likely inspired, but the working of these ministries in the Church is not always so neatly delineated. For instance, shepherds/pastors are those who care for the flock, yet all the ministries are called to shepherd the Church. All the true apostles listed in Scripture were shepherds, and both Paul and Peter exhorted the elders of the churches to shepherd the flock under their care.[58] Are we to believe that the only "Five-Folds" among all the elders of

---

[58] 1 Pet 5:1-4, Acts 20:28

these churches were pastors, and that there were no prophets, teachers, or evangelists? Were there no apostles residing in local churches or were they all on the road? Or could it be that when they were residing in the local church they were viewed as elders? According to Peter the answer is yes, since he refers to himself as a fellow elder.[59] So all church leaders are shepherds or pastors, yet it would seem there is a specific Five-Fold Ministry function of pastor. Also, Timothy, who was an apostle, was told by Paul to do the work of an evangelist. Was this because they needed an evangelist at the time, or because evangelism was part of the apostolic work? I think the latter because Paul adds "fulfill your ministry." So obviously, apostles are, or should also be, evangelists and all Biblical apostles evangelized the lost. Furthermore, all leaders must be able to teach[60] and handle the Word of God accurately[61] and all are exhorted to prophesy,[62] though not all are teachers or prophets.

When we compare the above examples of overlap revealed in Scripture with the teaching of the Apostolic Movement today, there is an unsettling lack of cohesiveness. We are usually presented with apostles as being distinct in gifting and function from the other ministries and having superior anointing. Yet in the Bible it seems that individuals who fulfilled the other ministries were called as apostles. So, there is a discrepancy. As we have seen already, the wildly popular NAR books argue that the church has been built around, and controlled by, pastors and teachers who have kept it immature and man-centered. The conclusion is that when apostles are back at the helm, the Church becomes heaven-focused because apostles bring heaven down. But this is preposterous since apostles in

---

[59] 1Pet 5:1
[60] 1Tim 3:2
[61] 2Tim 2:15
[62] 1Cor 14:1

Scripture were pastors, teachers and prophets, and most church planters and "recognized apostles" today started off as pastors of local churches.

Though we must get our teaching from what the Holy Spirit has revealed in Scripture, it is also important to evaluate what we see God doing in our experience. If it is Holy Spirit initiated, it will not contradict. And what we see today, and what we have seen in Church history, is that there is considerable overlap between the ministries -- a fact that most people who currently believe in the Five-Fold Ministry will readily admit. Most will use terms to explain this overlap such as a "prophetic teacher" or a "teaching apostle" or a "prophetic apostle" and so on. It is also clear from history and the experience of the Church today that no one starts off as an apostle unless they just declare themselves such, in which case it is usually received as a warning to stay away. Folks that become recognized as apostles usually start off as teachers, pastors, or prophets, or sometimes all of these. Indeed, although I am not certain it is a necessary qualification, they usually operate in more than one of the Five-Fold Ministries. There is not much evidence that evangelists become apostles, which is probably why no one "feels called" to be an evangelist anymore. Yet, when we look at the life of Charles Finney we can see a ministry that affected the whole Church. Also, the NAR itself, despite their own definition, in a somewhat bipolar fashion, has created so many types of apostles that the whole Church is now made up of apostles. As we said already, they have "vertical apostles," "horizontal apostles," "workplace apostles," "territorial apostles," "ambassadorial apostles," "convening apostles," and "presiding apostles" and the list keeps changing as they keep coming up with more ways to market their "apostolicity."

Conclusion

What then is the definition of an apostle? Are they church planters? They usually are but not exclusively, since pastors, prophets, teachers, and evangelists can all plant a local church and never venture out to plant another. Are they "wise master builders" according to 1Corintians 3:10? Well they should be, but it does not necessarily mean that they are. Indeed, that was Paul's point. He said he was a wise master builder because he laid the proper foundation, which was Jesus Christ, and he warned all other ministries to do the same. Again, since other ministries can lay the foundation, and even build on it, this cannot be the definition of an apostle. What we can say based on Scripture is this:

Apostles are sent by the Holy Spirit to the Church. This is what makes them apostles. They are called to the whole Church and are emissaries of Christ. They are concerned with the overall health of the Church and its relationship to Christ and its ministry in the world. They are usually seasoned individuals who carry the message of Christ, and are as certain as one can be of their calling and sending. They are individuals who possess some or all the other ministry giftings or functions. Some have more stature than others and a wider sphere. They all travel because they are sent, but when they are residing for a season in a local church they function as shepherds, elders or pastors.

Another thing, and perhaps the most important thing we should conclude regarding the Five-Fold Ministries, is that they are called to equip the Church and build it up and make it healthy by bringing the Body into maturity and unity in the Christian Faith, doctrine, experience and practice. The result being that the Bride is made ready for the Bridegroom, as well as properly reflecting the ministry of Jesus in the world.

Chapter Four
Structure & Alignment

"Some of the authors I read expressed certain frustrations because they found it difficult to get their arms around the NAR. They couldn't find a top leader or even a leadership team. There was no newsletter. The NAR didn't have an annual meeting. There was no printed doctrinal statement or code of ethics. This was very different from dealing with traditional denominations. The reason behind this is that, whereas denominations are legal structures, the NAR is a relational structure. Everyone is related to, or aligned, with an apostle or apostles. This alignment is voluntary. There is no legal tie that binds it. In fact, some have dual alignment or multiple alignment. Apostles are not in competition with each other, they are in cahoots. They do not seek the best for themselves, but for those who choose to align with them. If the spotlight comes on them, they will accept it, but they do not seek it."[63] *(Emphasis Mine)*

The above quote is taken from an article in *Charisma News* where Peter Wagner addresses the charge that the NAR is a cult. In his defense, he argues that the NAR does not have a legal structure, like denominations, but a relational one. This implies that the ministers in the movement are just friends who choose to align with one another voluntarily and are not bound together in any way. However, this is quite misleading since denominational pastors or leaders are not legally bound to their denomination. Surely their bonding is relational as well? While it is true that many are relationally bonded to the denomination itself rather than specific leaders, this does not mean that they are not free to leave and start their own work. Indeed, many

---

[63] C.P. Wagner, article in Charisma News, 8/24/2011 called *The New Apostolic Reformation Is Not a Cult*

pastors and even whole churches have! Of course, they must forfeit their ordination papers and whatever benefits they were enjoying in that denomination. Yet, the same is true for those who unalign themselves with the Apostolic Movement. Indeed, one could argue that the consequences will be costlier, since one who wishes to leave the NAR will be out of step with virtually all the mainstream Charismatic, Pentecostal and Revival networks. Nevertheless, although Wagner suggests the movement is merely relational, he admits there is a structure nonetheless.

Early Days of the Movement

Many try to link the NAR to the Latter Rain Movement of the late 1950's. There is truth to this, since the Latter Rain was focused on apostles and prophets. Nevertheless, it wasn't until the Charismatic Movement that the concept of the local church and the Five-Fold Ministry became commonplace. Many Charismatic leaders that had left the various denominations began to plant churches, and these churches often grew into groups or networks of churches. Thus, the label "Independent Charismatic." It was in these churches, throughout the 1980's, that the restoration of apostles and prophets and the Five-Fold Ministry emerged. Furthermore, the failure of the Shepherding/Discipleship Movement, with its unhealthy focus on "submission" and "covering," confirmed to many their desire to follow a "New Testament Model," which they viewed as strictly relational. These churches thrived, and by the end of the decade, they were the mainstream.

As is the case with all genuine revivals and restoration of Biblical truth, there was much human strife throughout this period, largely over the role and function of pastors and elders and Five-Fold Ministries. A multitude of teachers brought understanding to the movement, yet there was much disagreement on terms and roles. By the late 90's however, this confusion had mostly cleared, and there was wide acceptance of the function of apostles and prophets. Nevertheless, the movement was truly relational and organic and there was little abuse of titles. But all that was about to change!

Not an Organization?

C. Peter Wagner insisted that the NAR is not an organization, has no top leader, no team and no annual meeting. However, this is completely misleading and factually incorrect. Yes, there is no organization called the NAR with a president, a board and an annual meeting. However, there is an elaborate structure, carefully engineered by Wagner and his colleagues which they call the "new wineskin." This structure looks organic and fluid, but is highly organized and sophisticated -- as though it were designed by someone with high-level marketing skills. The wording is carefully crafted to appear and sound non-controlling or threatening, and Wagner admitted this many times. There is an above ground structure with strict membership and dues, and there is an underground structure which operates under the radar and establishes teachings, goals and strategies. Instead of boards, they have "councils" and "roundtables" that meet frequently, and a secret, private "inner circle" of apostles and prophets that are "covenanted" together. Each apostle and network is submitted to and under the covering of an apostle in the inner circle who is submitted to the "presiding apostle." However, they avoid the word "submission" and "covering" and instead speak of being "accountable" and "aligned."

Forming the "New Wineskin"

Peter Wagner was correct when he concluded that the Holy Spirit was raising up apostolic ministries and churches in the same way that He had done in the book of Acts. However, his theology and training led him to think that this work of the Holy

Spirit needed a name and a structure to accomplish its purpose. He kept referring to himself as merely a facilitator of what God was doing, but I think history will see it differently. In any event, Wagner settled on the name "The New Apostolic Reformation" in 1994.[64] He then recalls what happened next:

"Once I recognized that I had the spiritual gift of apostle, and particularly after my commissioning by the New Apostolic Roundtable, I found myself using more and more of my time in apostolic ministries. From time to time, for example, certain other apostles would approach me with requests that I agree to be their apostolic "covering." It took a while to work this through in prayer because I had no desire to become a vertical apostle. Over time, however, the Lord indicated that He wanted me to provide alignment (we have now found "alignment" to be a much more satisfactory term than "covering") to some fellow apostles. As I analyzed it, I concluded that the New Apostolic Roundtable was simply a fellowship group with no mechanism for formal alignment. In order to move forward, I then disbanded the New Apostolic Roundtable and organized Eagles Vision Apostolic Team (EVAT) in 2000. While some members moved from one to the other, some didn't. I agreed to provide primary apostolic alignment to those who decided to join EVAT, but I specified that it was an alignment with individuals only, not with the churches or networks or ministries that they represented. This is how I avoided establishing a pure vertical network. It obviously wasn't exactly a horizontal network either. I have sometimes thought about calling it a 'diagonal network.' In order to seal the covenant relationship, EVAT members agreed to contribute a monthly sum toward my salary and benefits.... We keep in touch through an annual meeting, as well as through seeing each other frequently during the year.

---

[64] C.P. Wagner, article in Charisma News, 8/24/2011, called *The New Apostolic Reformation Is Not a Cult*

I set the membership limit at 25, and this is the closest apostolic group to whom Doris and I relate."[65]

Here we have laid out for us the formation of the NAR and it is anything but loosely organized or merely relational. In fact, we are told that the group which was relational or "horizontal," had no mechanism for "formal alignment" and therefore Wagner disbanded it. Some didn't join the new group. I wonder why? Obviously, they wanted relationship but not "formal alignment." So "formal alignment" is way more than relationship because it consists of commitment and submission to the "presiding apostle," being under his authority, tithing to him, and making some kind of oath.[66] "Alignment," of course, sounds so much better than all that, but it doesn't change the reality of what's happening. Wagner then goes into full pretense, admitting it's a vertical arrangement under his apostleship, and then jokingly tries to skew it horizontally to make him and his colleagues feel better. However, this EVAT team led by Mr. Wagner became the secret leadership of the whole NAR movement and all who "align" with it. From this he and his associates would create, or align, a host of "councils" and "roundtables" and "networks" that appear independent, but are all formally aligned with each other and EVAT. It is a strategy like that of the EU or the UN. With a vast array of networks and organizations, there is the appearance of voluntary unity and individual freedom. Yet, they are all given the same teaching and talking points, are accountable to the same sources and individuals, and all work together for the agenda of the movement. It's very clever, really, and hard for

---

[65] *Wrestling with Alligators, Prophets, and Theologians: Lessons from a Lifetime in the Church – A Memoir*, By C. Peter Wagner, by Regal Books

[66] We know from videos of alignments, available on the Internet, that oaths are administered such as; "I agree with, and promise to, etc." Since this is so, it is not unreasonable to assume that "formal alignment" with EVAT, which is secret, involves an oath.

individual pastors or churches to identify until they have already drank the Kool-Aid.

ICAL (International Coalition of Apostolic Leaders)

"While EVAT provides my deepest apostolic relationships, The International Coalition of Apostles (ICA) provides the broadest. I have built ICA on the model of a professional society of pier-level, mutually recognized apostles. Up to 400 apostles, 25% of whom live outside of the United States, have agreed to pay dues, attend an annual meeting and adhere to the professional standards of Christian apostles…. ICA came about as a result of a spontaneous meeting of several apostles in Singapore in 1999. I do not have a record of all that were there, but I am sure of Ed Silvoso, Lawrence Khong, and John Kelly. They all agreed that there should be some organization that brought apostles together, and John Kelly was the one who picked up the ball and established the first ICA office in Ft. Worth, Texas. While Kelly, a vertical apostle, was the founder of ICA, he soon recognized that my gift of horizontal apostle might be more effective in running the organization than his, so he invited me to become ICA's presiding apostle. We then moved the office to Colorado Springs under Global Harvest Ministries."[67] (Emphasis Mine)

It appears than John Kelly started ICA or ICAL as it is known today. However, it was soon handed over to C.P. Wagner, who was, as it appears, involved all along. He says he built it on the model of a professional society and makes it clear that it is an organization of "mutually recognized" apostles. These apostles agree to attend annual meetings, pay dues, and adhere to certain "professional standards," whatever they might be.

---

[67] *Wrestling with Alligators, Prophets, and Theologians: Lessons from a Lifetime in the Church – A Memoir*, By C. Peter Wagner, Regal Books

It is astonishing to me that leaders, who claim to promote Biblical restoration of the Church would be so quick to sign up with something so clearly and admittedly unscriptural. Honestly, a professional society? A secret apostolic team? Such things are condemned in Scripture. Where does the New Testament advocate the need to join a private elite club of apostles, pay dues, and be "recognized" by them to be a legitimate minister? This is ludicrous. Certainly, Paul would not have joined. See his comments to the Galatians:[68]

"For am I now seeking the favor of men, or of God? Or am I striving to please men? If I were still trying to please men, I would not be a bond-servant of Christ."

The Apostles in the New Testament were adamant that they were called by God and credentialed by Him alone. They taught us to be at peace with others and work together as much as possible,[69] yet never to seek the approval of man, but of God. Now however, ICAL insists that to be a member of their professional society, apostles must be recognized by their peers, recommended by two members, and then they can join the club. And presumably, if they want to stay recognized, they must attend an annual meeting, pay hefty dues,[70] and be in a perpetual state of alignment with their aligned apostle. ICAL, of course, insists that they are not a "covering" agency, while at the same time they are "relational and accountable to one another." They are trying to suggest that they merely exist for mutual accountability. However, once again, this is misleading. They have made commitments, are paying dues, and are accountable to the organization and its leaders. They are

---

[68] Gal 1:1,10, 2:6

[69] Rom 12:18

[70] $450 annually to be a resident apostle, $650 if you're married, and $350 if you are an international apostle or a First Nations (American Indian) apostle

aligned with the apostles in ICAL and its "presiding apostle," which is aligned with EVAT and its "presiding apostle," who happens to be the same person. And we know that "alignment" is merely a nicer, more politically correct word for "covering." It's just a clever game of semantics that seems to be very effective in bringing the whole Church under their influence and control.

Jesus and the Apostles warned us about lording it over others and thereby shot down the notion of a hierarchy of professionals under a "presiding apostle." Yet the NAR, while all the while denying it, has brought multitudes of churches and networks under the influence of a pyramid of apostles, all aligned and covenanted to each other, and the "presiding apostle," who is the functional equivalent of a bishop or pope. So far there are no robes and rings and miters, but it is the same type of denominational structure that looks organic and relational on the surface, but underneath are the ceremonies and trappings of a secret society. This is the "New Apostolic Age," the "New Wineskin" for the Church today that began, according to its founders, when EVAT and ICAL were organized at the turn of the 21st Century.

The Tentacles of Alignment
Somewhere around 2007 or 2008, the NAR revealed its structure and goals in a very specific way. Since then much of this information has been removed from the internet. Nevertheless, once it's on the internet it is hard to completely remove. It is harder to find, and some pieces have gone entirely; yet there is still sufficient information to outline the declared strategy of the movement. The following chart put out by what

was, at the time, Global Harvest Ministries,[71] appeared and can still be found with a simple Google search.

The organizations on the chart and some of the players have changed slightly since it was produced, yet the strategy revealed has continued much the same. The Kingdom of God, which appears on the top, is established on earth by the infiltration and domination of the so-called "7 Mountains or Molders of Culture." These "7 Mountains," usually referred to as the "7M's," are taken over by the religion mountain which of

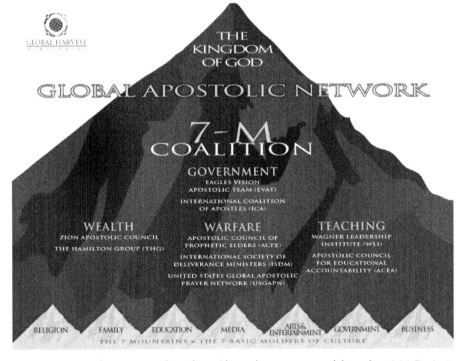

course is taken over by the Church governed by the NAR. It is, as I have been saying, a pyramid structure under EVAT and ICAL.

---

[71] GHM was the ministry of C.P. Wagner and the governmental leadership of the NAR. It was replaced in 2010 by Global Spheres when Chuck Pierce replaced Wagner as the Presiding Apostle over the movement.

The next layer of the pyramid is broken into the three main arms of the NAR in its strategy to conquer the 7M's and bring in the Kingdom. They are: Wealth, Warfare and Teaching. Under each heading there is a list of organizations (all founded either directly or indirectly by C.P.Wagner) that will seek to accomplish each goal. In the Wealth column are the organizations that will facilitate the "great transfer of wealth" to the Church, which Mr. Wagner said was coming and was needed to bring in the Kingdom. These are: Zion Apostolic Council and the Hamilton Group and another not mentioned in the chart -- the **Apostolic Council for Kingdom Wealth**. Under the Warfare heading, we see listed the Apostolic Council of Prophetic Elders (ACPE -- currently led by Cindy Jacobs) which aligns the prophetic movement and the various intercessor networks and keeps them focused on the NAR agenda. Then we have the International Society of Deliverance Ministries (ISDM) originally led by Doris Wagner and now by Bill and Janet Sudduth. This group works to align all deliverance and healing ministries. The last one listed is the United Apostolic Global Prayer Network (USGAPN) which was given to Chuck Pierce, who, according to Mr. Wagner, disbanded it and "opened the gates for the formation of a variety of new networks providing alignment for many aspects of Kingdom ministry."[72]

The 3rd arm of the NAR is under the heading "Teaching," and it consists of the Wagner Leadership Institute (WLI) and the Apostolic Council for Educational Accountability (ACEA). WLI, which is currently run by Che Ahn, trains and credentials pastors (and of course apostles) through courses available online, that unabashedly promote the teaching and agenda of the NAR as curriculum. Many "Spirit-filled" pastors who feel the need for

---

[72]C. Peter Wagner letter from Global Harvest Ministries, July 11, 2008, *News from Global Harvest Ministries*, subtitled *Alignment! Looking toward the Future*. (This letter is difficult to find now)

credentials and training take these courses and become aligned with the NAR whether they meant to or not. The ACEA, on the other hand, is an organization which provides an alternative to traditional academic accreditation and is currently led by its presiding apostle, Leo Lawson. Bible schools and church schools find accreditation and "accountability" in this organization, and there is also a list of distinguished "society professionals" who also have membership.

All the organizations mentioned in the Global Apostolic Network chart are led by EVAT members, and there are others that are not mentioned. Their goal is to align all the various spheres of Christian ministry under the NAR apostles and networks so that they can execute the 7M Mandate. This was stated clearly by Mr. Wagner in a letter from Global Harvest Ministries that appeared on the website in July 2008.

"Through the 1990s and up until recently, my major vehicle for providing alignment for the prayer movement was what ultimately became known as the U.S. Global Apostolic Prayer Network (USGAPN). I assigned Cindy Jacobs to lead this for a season, then transitioned to Chuck Pierce. At the beginning of 2008, Chuck stepped down and dissolved the USGAPN. This was a huge step forward because it opened the gates for the formation of a variety of new networks providing alignment for many aspects of kingdom ministry. Let me just mention several of the newer networks being led by apostles who are members of my inner circle, Eagles Vision Apostolic Team (EVAT). These developments show that the wineskins of the past must give way to wineskins of the future:

· John Kelly has founded the International Christian Wealth Builders Foundation (ICWBF).

· Cindy Jacobs has founded the Reformation Prayer Network (RPN) and the Deborah Company.

· Ché Ahn has formed the Revival Alliance.

· Dutch Sheets has launched the U.S. Apostolic Alliance (USAA).

· Tommi Femrite has started the Apostolic Intercessors Network (AIN).

· Barbara Wentroble has initiated the Breakthrough Business Network (BBN).

· Robert Henderson leads the Freedom Apostolic Alliance.

· Mel Mullen is introducing new thrusts and emphases to his Life Church Network.

· John Benefiel continues to build the Heartland Apostolic Prayer Network."[73] (Emphasis Mine)

Since this letter was written, more organizations and networks have been established such as EAL (European Apostolic Alliance) under Jan-Aage Torp, and the AAC (Association of Apostolic Centers), founded by Wagner in January, 2015. All of them are connected directly to EVAT and either directly or indirectly to the various networks and roundtables. This strategy has been very successful when it comes to taking over the Church. So much so, that it is hard to find a Christian ministry or network that has not been aligned.

The Apostolic Delivery System

The NAR has much to say about its intended goal of "taking dominion" over the earth. But for now, it is little more than talk. No countries, or cities, or villages, or even enclaves, have yet been taken or have become obedient to the Kingdom. All the real action is taking place inside the Church, which is being seduced by an elaborate and multi-pronged strategy that is

---

[73]C. Peter Wagner letter from Global Harvest Ministries, July 11, 2008, *News from Global Harvest Ministries*, subtitled *Alignment! Looking toward the Future*. (This letter is difficult to find now)

difficult to identify. Upon careful examination, however, there is a blueprint that can be seen and it all traces back to the same persons and organizations whether directly or indirectly. This is the genius of the movement -- its underground structure that is held together by the magic of alignment.

- Talking Points

    When political parties and organizations want everybody to be on the same page, they release something they call "talking points." This is usually a list of Instructions about what to emphasize, how to explain it, how to answer questions, and which buzzwords to use. Common sense tells us that when a bunch of people all around the world start using the same words and phrases at the same time, they have all gotten the memo. However, to Christians, unaware of the source of the memo, it is a sign that they are all hearing from God. Furthermore, when prophets, who are the mouthpieces of the NAR (and who usually become the apostles), are believed to be speaking from God, their "words from the Lord" have great sway over churches and leaders.

- Media

    In the late 80's and early 90's, I read a lot of books by various authors with a view to a better understanding of what God was doing in the Church. I am not one to read the introduction (although I plead with you to read mine), but I always look at the endorsements. I couldn't help but notice that almost every book I picked up had a foreword by C.P. Wagner. I never knew what this was about until I began to understand the NAR. Whoever wants to publish a book and get it sold covets a NAR signature on the cover. This trend, coupled with the alignment of many teachers and publishers with the NAR, guarantees the movement control over the print media. There are some publishers and distributors that are openly aligned, such as: Charisma, the Elijah List, and Destiny Image, but others are so influenced by its teacher's popularity and influence, that they have become mouthpieces. If you doubt what I say, then I challenge you to get them to advertise this book, or any book that confronts their teaching. Also, TV stations such as; God TV, TBN, and Daystar have essentially been taken over by NAR and Word of Faith preachers. Most recently, the NAR has begun its own channels which will spread its agenda to the masses.

- Roundtables & Councils

    A vast network of "Apostolic and Prophetic Roundtables," based on EVAT and ACPE and aligned with the NAR, are being established all over the world. Some are vocal and can be found on the web, although times, locations and invitations are always private. They are presumably regional, but since they are secret, they are impossible to locate and identify. It is all being presented as "spontaneous" and "organic," and pastors and leaders who mostly crave peer-level friendship are lured and often flattered into joining. After all, who doesn't want to feel part of something bigger where their ministries are recognized, and where they can input the agenda?

    "The 'Round Table' is to be a place where the ministries of Christ, Apostles and Prophets, these being foundational, can sit together to participate in the Divine Council regarding the affairs of mankind. It is to be a place where men and women from different cultures, styles and backgrounds can celebrate their

commonalities and participate in their diversity. All can listen and contribute to the counsel, participating with heaven's movements on earth. It will be a place where God can ask the question 'whom can I send?'"[74]

The above quote comes from Gareth Duffty of Together Ministries in Coventry, England, and I chose it because it illustrates the attractiveness of the roundtables. Many assume that all these apostles and prophets are on the same page theologically, but that is not the case. It's a mistake to think that Biblical theology is what unites the movement. On the contrary, they celebrate diversity of views. It is relationship, alignment, and a common belief in the transformation of the Church and the world, through the ministry of apostles and prophets. This is what motivates and excites them. This shared view of apostles and prophets is the foundation, and relational alignment is the glue that holds them together. And of course, the apostolic roundtable is a means of spreading the virus. Many are convinced that all this is happening spontaneously by the work of the Holy Spirit, and that all are peers without anyone "in control." At the same time, they feel secure in their alignment with other apostles, who are in turn aligned with others, all the way back to ICAL and EVAT. The only explanation for this bi-polar behavior is the common belief that they are in a "New Apostolic Age." After all, the apostles that have been recognized and approved by so many must be close to perfect, as were the Twelve, and therefore healed of all fleshly desires to control and manipulate. What happened to the Shepherding Movement won't happen

---

[74]Gareth Duffty,
http://togetherweb.net/together/index.php/about-us/apostolic-round-table/92-together-web/about-us/apostolic-round-table/88

to them! No way! They are far more careful and sophisticated. However, whatever mistakes were made in the Shepherding Movement, the NAR is the Fort Lauderdale Five[75] on mega steroids.

- **Conferences**

  Regional and national conferences are perhaps the primary means of spreading the NAR doctrine and goals. They are like political rallies where the apostles and prophets stir up and energize the crowds who generally spend big money to attend. In fact, many Christians live in a sort of conference euphoria, chasing after the popular speakers who are like rock stars, and parroting the latest "cool revelation." This often creates a false sense of reality for the speakers as well as the attendees, by giving the impression that the world is being transformed. Nevertheless, these rallies spread the message and sell the books that impact local churches and pastors, who are often needing support and encouragement.

- **Apostolic Centers**

  Through the Charismatic Movement God began to establish local churches instead of denominations or institutions. Believers gathered together under local leadership in the same way they did in the Early Church.

"When they had appointed elders for them in every church, having prayed with fasting, they commended them to the Lord in whom they had believed." Acts 14:23

---

[75]The Fort Lauderdale Five was often used to refer to the five ministries that founded Christian Growth Ministries (CGM) of Ft. Lauderdale FL, which became known as the Discipleship Movement.

It is true that these early believers embraced the ministry of the Apostles ordained by the Lord, but it is also clear that they sometimes received false apostles as well. They were frequently addressed by their locality such as, "the church in Rome" or "the church in Corinth." Thus, we see the proof that they were viewed as autonomous local assemblies and not as under some hierarchy instituted by Jerusalem. Extra local ministries were either received or rejected based on their message and stature in the faith, and not because they were presently occupying some pre-established office of president, director, or presiding apostle.

As we have seen already, the NAR, although it presents the ideal of relational authority, is actually a hierarchical structure composed of networks and councils that are "under" a person or group of persons. Indeed, they frequently use the term "under" when referring to their "relational" structure. In recent years, however, the movement has begun to create what they call "apostolic centers" which they claim are more Biblical and "apostolic" than local churches. Peter Wagner's apparent last assignment was to align apostolic centers with something he called the Association of Apostolic Centers (AAC) -- more alignment.

There is nothing inherently wrong with the idea of an apostolic center. Many local churches are apostolic centers that are equipping and sending people and planting new churches. This should be the vision for all local churches. Nevertheless, when a distinction is made between a local church and an apostolic center, with the latter presented as more Biblical and a "new wineskin," it amounts to undermining the local church. The NAR leaders are quick to say we still need local churches, but when they describe their focus and function, it's hard to imagine why we would need them. The following is a list of distinctions attributed to C.P. Wagner and spread about by various networks and websites.[76]

Local Churches (Typical church)	**Apostolic Centers** (Ekklesia)
Self-Centered (people & church)	Kingdom Centered
Small Vision	Vision for the Future
Spiritual Birth Control	Aggressive Propagation
Avoid the Devil	Attack the Devil
Bedroom Worship	Throne Room Worship
Intimacy	Industry (Production)
Loveaholics	Workaholics
Feminine	Masculine
For Maintenance	For Outreach
Profile - More passive and peaceful, weaker	More aggressive and stronger
Leadership style is conformity	Leadership style is creativity
Prayer - Petition, self needs	Decreeing and Kingdom needs
Revelation - Interpret the written word	Written word and prophecy
Focus - On the Congregation	On the kingdom
Government – Pastor Cares for Needs	Apostle – mobilizes people
Staff- Pastors & Teachers	Apostle, Prophet, Pastors, Teachers, Evangelist

All social expectations must be met, worship, prayer, care, etc. This comes natural.	All social expectations must be met, worship, prayer, care, etc. This must be worked at.

The above list is not very flattering for local churches and pastors. But then, we have already established in chapter 2 that they view pastors and teachers unfavorably. And these are the ones who they say lead "typical churches." There is, however, one plus in the local church column --

---

[76] https://www.gloryofzion.org/docs/Apostolic%20Centers_sm.pdf,

"social expectations." Apparently local churches do a better job taking care of people's needs and apostolic centers must "work at" this. This is not surprising, of course, since the NAR sees the church as a means to an end, rather than a family that exists for Christ.[77] But it is also somewhat amusing, since the apostolic center supposedly exists for "social transformation."

It is fair to say that many churches are not apostolic and should be. It is also true that leaders who have more of a Biblical worldview will have churches that are more apostolic, even apostolic centers. But the local church is the work of Christ and exists for Christ. No one has the right to denigrate it or undermine it. Furthermore, despite the weaknesses of local churches, they are the primary means of evangelism in every city. People are coming to Christ in local churches, and though the ministry they receive is often inadequate, true apostles don't undermine this work. I know of pastors who, because of NAR indoctrination, have dismantled their churches and scattered their congregations to establish "apostolic centers." This is scandalous and no true shepherd would ever allow it. We need to be giving ourselves to helping local churches become strong and not dismantling them. However, it seems that the NAR seeks to undermine local churches and marginalize and delegitimize their leaders who won't submit to their agenda and align themselves with their apostles.

---

[77] Titus 2:14, Acts 20:26,1Pet 5:2

Some quotes on apostolic centers:

"Last week I sent a personal letter indicating that God is doing a new thing. Our local church, HRock, our international apostolic network, HIM, and our seminary and training center, WLI, are merging into Harvest Apostolic Center (HAC). Being an apostolic center is not a form of reorganization; it is a new wineskin, an entirely new way of being the Church and advancing God's Kingdom."[78]

"Generally speaking, the typical contemporary local congregation has no vision beyond the care and concern for their own flock and adding to their membership. Even if a church has an apostolic vision to release fivefold ministers (Ephesians 4:11) to serve the greater body of Christ, most of these churches have basically sent out their Set One (senior pastor or bishop) as an apostolic leader. But the local church often has very little connection with the Set One who was sent out and (consequently) the local church becomes autonomous from outside interference and/or apostolic governance."[79]

"To activate the transformation of local churches into apostolic centers and link them into apostolic networks in order to establish alignment for territorial transformation."[80]

---

[78] *A New Wineskin* by Ché Ahn, http://hrockchurch.com/blog/new-wineskin

[79] Joseph Mattera, *What Makes Today's Church Different from the Apostolic Church?* Charisma News 7/11/2014

[80] Quote attributed to Alain Caron, https://www.gloryofzion.org/docs/Apostolic%20Centers_sm.pdf,

- ## The Magic of Alignment

  "A large part of the apostolic ministry to which God has called me is facilitating Biblical alignment. When the Bible says that apostles (and others) are to "equip" the saints for the work of ministry, the literal meaning of "equip" is "align."[81]

  In the early days of the NAR, Peter Wagner mentioned that he came up with the word "alignment" as a better alternative to "covering."[82] Later however, he began to teach that the Greek word *katartismon* used in Ephesians 4:12, and translated as "equip" in our Bibles, was about being "aligned" with the apostles. Now that teaching is everywhere. Consider this article from the NAR mouthpiece *Charisma*:

  "I do believe in alignment and accountability. The Bible teaches alignment, which is the concept of coming alongside, but not over, others. Alignment is also a Biblical word. It's used several times in the New Testament. 'For the equipping of the saints, for the work of service, ...' (Eph. 4:12). This word equipping is 'katartizo' in the Greek and it means 'alignment or to put a thing in its proper position.' The purpose of the five-fold ministry is to align you or position you for the work of the ministry. Alignment increases your authority to function in Christ's kingdom."[83]

---

[81] C. Peter Wagner letter from Global Harvest Ministries, July 11, 2008, *News from Global Harvest Ministries*, subtitled *Alignment! Looking toward the Future.* (This letter is difficult to find now)

[82] The word "covering" is from the "Discipleship or Shepherding" movement era and tends to be associated with "control."

[83] Ken Malone, *4 Natural and Spiritual Benefits of Apostolic Alignment*, Charisma News, 9/27/2015

The word *katartismon* is a masculine noun and is used only one time in the New Testament, and that is in Ephesians 4:12. The word is translated "equipping, perfecting or completing." The verb *katartizo*, from which it comes, has the following meanings:

1) to render, i.e. to fit, sound, complete
1a) to mend (what has been broken or rent), to repair
1a1) to complete
1b) to fit out, equip, put in order, arrange, adjust
1b1) to fit or frame for one' s self, prepare
1c) ethically: to strengthen, perfect, complete, make one what he ought to be[84]

Thus, *katartismon* can be translated "equipping, perfecting, or even mending" the saints. In the Gospels, it is used with James and John "mending" their nets, and in New Testament times it also had a medical usage, such as setting bones. Can it be translated "alignment?" Perhaps in the sense of putting things straight or in order, but it is extremely misleading to suggest that it means relationship with an apostle, or any other of the ministries listed. That is ridiculous and an absolute distortion of the text. Christ is the foundation. We are aligned with Him. He is the cornerstone from whom the whole building or body (as in the context) gets its proper order and function. The Five-Fold Ministries mentioned are to bring us into maturity in Christ, and to a unity in the Christian faith, so we will not be tossed here and there by winds of false doctrines and the trickery of men. To suggest that aligning oneself with an apostle or movement constitutes this "equipping or perfecting" is the type of trickery and

---

[84] Thayers Greek Lexicon

craftiness being spoken against. It is taking advantage of those who are ignorant of the Word, and who cannot discern that they are being directed toward human relationships for security, rather than Christ.

This deceptive teaching on alignment, especially when it comes from "recognized apostles," is difficult to discern, especially when they stress "it is a coming alongside, but not over, others." Really? One "aligns" with an apostle (or several apostles who are aligned with each other) and takes an oath of alignment, comes "under" their ministry, is accountable to them, is in "covenant" with them (and it is not just the New Covenant), and it is all just brotherly or fatherly relationship? Who in their right mind believes that? This is crafty double-speak, designed to deceive, and it is how the NAR holds it all together while taking over churches and movements.

Apostolic Succession

Since I began to write this book, C.P. Wagner, the father of the NAR movement, has passed away. However, since 2010, his role as presiding apostle has been transferred to Chuck D. Pierce. Together, they founded Global Spheres specifically for this purpose. Chuck, who is now called an apostle, is the new presiding apostle of the NAR. Of course, it's not written down anywhere quite like that, but one must know the language and put it all together. Remember, they are masters with words and marketing techniques. Why Global Spheres? They are presenting a new name and a new identity, giving the allusion that it is not papal succession, when it actually is. Indeed, they even admit that it is.

"When we go, there will be no need for transition because it is Chuck's organization, incorporated in the State of Texas. What

is Global Spheres? Much of the answer to this question will become clear over the next few months as we work out the details. Meanwhile, GSI is focused on alignment. As the apostolic movement has mushroomed, an increasing number of leaders are recognizing that they lack formal apostolic alignment, and they are actively seeking it. Both Chuck and I receive frequent appeals from other apostles and prophets, as well as from evangelists, pastors, teachers, and workplace leaders for us to provide necessary alignment. How can this be provided? One very public example of this is the recent apostolic alignment of Evangelist Todd Bentley with the Revival Alliance. While we applaud that stream, we realize that if we are going to be looking to the future, we in our stream must also provide a comparable vehicle. One size does not fit all!"[85]

On the Global Spheres website, under the title, "*Mantles must be passed and proper succession must occur in each generation,*" we find the following:

"*One of the most difficult transitions to make is the passing of a mantle from one generation to its next successor. When Peter approached me regarding Global Harvest Ministries, I knew that the Lord was saying something to me but I was not sure how to proceed. I knew there were areas in GHM that I should eventually assume leadership of but I knew I was not just to take this ministry, become President, and attempt to carry forth its administration. I knew that I could represent Peter and Doris as a good son in certain facets, but not all, of their ministry. Since I have known Peter and Doris, I have also served as President of Glory of Zion International Ministries in Denton, Texas. I knew that I was not to absorb GHM into this wineskin which is more*

---

[85]C. Peter Wagner letter from Global Harvest Ministries, July 11, 2008, *News from Global Harvest Ministries*, subtitled *Alignment! Looking toward the Future.* (This letter is difficult to find now)

prophetic in nature and aligned with God's call to form "One New Man," Jew and Gentile. The passing of a mantle and development of new wineskins dictates the creation of a new administration with new methods of development." (Emphasis Mine)

Since it was all taken care of back in 2010, there is no need for the public to see any transition or succession taking place. It's all on a need to know basis. Pierce is now the head but they will never call him that. They may even call him something other than presiding apostle for a while, just to let everyone get used to it. Remember, this is a "new wineskin" flexing as it goes. But those who are aligned may know, or not know. Who cares, so long as they are "properly aligned?"

"Specifically, what kind of alignment does GSI offer? Chuck Pierce is widely recognized as a prophet, but he is an apostle as well. Peter Wagner has a substantial track record as an apostle and also a teacher. This means that those who choose to identify with Global Spheres thus become aligned with apostle, prophet, and teacher, numbers one, two, and three in the divine order for the government of the church as seen in 1 Corinthians 12:28 quoted above. GSI is not a church or a substitute for a church. It is not designed to provide pastoral care to members of the body of Christ in general. All believers should be under the care of a pastor, hopefully a pastor who has secured proper apostolic alignment. GSI is an apostolic network which provides proper apostolic alignment to leaders."[86] (Emphasis Mine)

Here we are introduced to a new phrase -- "proper alignment." Now what does that mean? Well, it can only mean that you are not "properly aligned" unless your apostle is approved of or

---

[86] From the Global Spheres Network website, Prospectus
http://globalspheres.org/prospectus.asp

traceable to their "inner circle." Are you starting to get the "willies?" How wrong it is for them to pass judgment on other servants of God, people they don't even know, simply because they are not "under them," or "recognized" by their streams? Do they really think that God has placed them over the Church? How dare they undermine other pastors and churches who are humbly walking with Jesus! Perhaps they need to consider what Paul, one of the greatest apostles ever, had to say about how we are not to judge other servants of God.

"Who are you to judge the servant of another? To his own master he stands or falls; and he will stand, for the Lord is able to make him stand." Rom 14:4

"Let a man regard us in this manner, as servants of Christ and stewards of the mysteries of God. In this case, moreover, it is required of stewards that one be found trustworthy. But to me it is a very small thing that I may be examined by you, or by any human court; in fact, I do not even examine myself. For I am conscious of nothing against myself, yet I am not by this acquitted; but the one who examines me is the Lord. Therefore do not go on passing judgment before the time, but wait until the Lord comes who will both bring to light the things hidden in the darkness and disclose the motives of men's hearts; and then each man's praise will come to him from God." 1 Cor 4:1-5

Wagner indicated that when he died, EVAT would be no more. What he meant was they would no longer be aligned with him and would not be called by that name. Thus, EVAT is no more. But I can assure you that they were also aligned with Pierce, and that the "inner circle" which needs no public name, is alive and well.

But They Are Such Good People?

When folks are confronted with the structure and strategy of these new apostles, their first reaction is usually one of defensiveness and disbelief. They respond with, "But they are such good people." And, of course, they are. That is the whole point. These are God's people and many of them are powerful lovers and ministers of Christ. How then could they be involved in or promote something so obviously man-centered? The answer is very simple. Who else would the enemy try to deceive? Surely he wouldn't use this kind of bait on bad people? Not at all. That would be a waste of time. This scheme is carefully designed for church leaders and has been successfully used on them before. It's called bait and switch. They are being baited by their passion for success, influence, dominion, control, authority and power. It's being fed to them on gold-plated skewers, laced with Bible verses, and promises of revival, awakening, and of course miracles. The key to success, that was there all along, has at last been discovered -- apostles. All one must do is align and the blessings of authority will start to flow. And with so many jumping on board -- so many famous people -- who wants to be left behind? How can there be anything wrong with something so big, so organized, so popular, so successful? Who wants to miss the Kingdom train -- the destiny of God?

Dear Friends, you may be asking, "If this is the bait then when does the switch come?" Don't worry, it will come soon enough. The NAR train is heading somewhere but it is not heaven on earth. In the next few chapters we will discuss the destination of the train and the weeping and gnashing of teeth that will ensue from its derailment. But for now, it is time to recognize that we are living in a time of great sifting worldwide. It is the end of the age and the Great Apostasy is upon us. Don't be surprised that God sifts you. He allows all His people to be sifted and especially His leaders. The fire of God will purify a remnant for Himself.

"But who can endure the day of His coming? And who can stand when He appears? For He is like a refiner's fire and like fullers' soap." Mal 3:2-3

Conclusion

As I close this chapter, I want to say to all the "aligned" out there that what you are doing is wrong. If you participated in a ceremony where you were "formally" or "properly aligned," you need to repent. What you did was wrong. Yes, we are to follow and submit to godly leaders, but we are not to pledge allegiance or take oaths to other individuals.[87] And by the way, a promise spoken before God is an oath. It is bad enough that you placed yourself in this alignment, but you also did it to the members of your church and network. Do your people know what you have done? Do your church or network members know who or what they are submitted to? And if not, what right do you have to conceal it from them? What right do you have to be secretive about what you have done, and what the people you have placed yourself under are doing? Oh, I'm sure their names are known to your church or network, and they are familiar with the teaching because of you, but do they know what is happening in secret? You are being deceptive and fraudulent towards them and you need to come clean. Even the world considers this type of behavior to be wrong. And though I am no fan of denominations, at least with them you know what you are getting into, what they believe, and who is guiding the ship. But your people think it's you. They joined your church or network to follow you and you have deceived them. Turn to God and repent and speak truth to your people. Stop withholding

---

[87] Mt 5:34-37

91

from them the reality that you are following someone or something else. This does not mean leaders need to tell their followers everything that goes on in private, but they have a right to know who they are following. Stop lying to yourself and them by saying, "We are just friends." You know it's way more than that. Perhaps you think because all is going so well for you, and the blessings are flowing, that God is pleased with your secret arrangement. But I can assure you a time of reckoning is coming.

As we have examined the NAR structure, we have seen the layers of networks and the alignment glue that holds them all together. On the surface, the Body of Christ seems mesmerized by its "deep revelations" and "spontaneous" unity. Indeed, it's a glowing mountain of Kingdom sparkle and divine activity. However, its real strength and effectiveness lies in its secret caverns and underground systems that are by invitation only. While it rails against denominations and their "old wineskin" structures, it plunges the unsuspecting believers and churches into a medieval system of knights and roundtables and secret ordinations of the ruling elites. And since all the well-knowns have been initiated, there is no one to cry out -- no one to challenge its doctrines or freshly prophesied mysteries. But sooner or later many will wake up. They will come to their senses and realize they have seen all this before -- councils, bishops, cardinals, conventions and the Apostolic See (Vatican). There is nothing new under the sun.

Chapter Five
Present Truth?

When I first heard the term "present truth" many years ago, it was used rather innocently to try to explain what the Holy Spirit was emphasizing today, and not some new extra-Biblical teaching. Over time, we began to use the term "restored truth" which is much more accurate. Although for us who believe the Bible and live by its teaching there is no "new truth," only truth that has already existed in Scripture which we have not known or understood. There are, of course, cultural differences from Biblical times, and we must extract Biblical principles and apply them to these circumstances, yet truth remains the same. The Bible is clear that it is the sole source of truth, that it is inspired by God, and that it cannot be altered or improved upon.[88] In other words, there are no movable goalposts.

It is true to say that NAR apostles, at least those in the inner circle, are steadfast in their belief that the moral teaching of Scripture cannot be altered or reinterpreted. Yet, when it comes to what the Church should teach, or how it is to be governed, or how it should act in the world, there seems to be much more latitude. Indeed, one can say that, by and large, the movement has already embraced the concept of a moving goalpost with the idea of a "new wineskin." If Jesus' ministry and practice, which He passed on to His disciples was a new wineskin,[89] then it is still the only wineskin which can be used today. Nevertheless, Mr. Wagner successfully planted the notion in his

---

[88] 2 Tim 3:16

[89] It can be argued whether Jesus was saying that His teaching was a new wineskin or not. For instance, in Luke's account the phrase is added, "And no one, after drinking old *wine* wishes for new; for he says, 'The old is good *enough.*'" Thus, the Lord may have been saying that His practice was the old wine, which was the practice of the prophets and patriarchs, and the Pharisee's legalistic attitude was new wine that did not belong in the old wineskin of Biblical Judaism.

apostles that the New Testament wineskin that Jesus gave His disciples is itself an old wineskin, and the NAR has received a new one for today. Thus, they take principles and lingo from the Church established by Jesus, and interject them into a new 21st Century structure, that they claim can do what the Early Church failed to do -- transform culture and bring heaven to earth.[90] This is all justified by the concept of "present truth."

Apostles Determine Doctrine

The Apostles of the Lord made it clear that Scripture alone was the only source for doctrine and theology.[91] Unless what was being said or done harmonized with the Word, it was to be rejected. They studied the Scriptures daily to understand the heart and will of God. When there was a dispute in the Church concerning the Gentiles being saved, which seemed to some to go against Scripture, they convened a meeting in Jerusalem. The conclusion of that meeting was not a new word, or *rhema*, but the simple conclusion that the salvation of Gentiles in Messiah was promised in Scripture, and they should accept it. They wrote a letter to the Gentile converts explaining this and only asked for them to follow some pastoral guidelines. This does not suggest that these leaders were not hearing what the Holy Spirit was saying to them at the time. On the contrary, they were in continual communion with Him, yet they never considered their revelation or experiences alone to be the proof of authenticity. Scripture alone was the plumbline, or measuring rod, for determining what was of God and what was against His will. This is clearly demonstrated by Paul when he told the Galatians that even if an angel from heaven were to bring a gospel different to what he gave them, he was to be accursed.[92]

---

[90] "*For the most part, believers did not have the power to transform the society of the Roman Empire, where most of them found themselves.*" (Quote from: *The Church in the Workplace: How God's People Can Transform Society*, by C. Peter Wagner, pg. 38

[91] 2Tim 3:16

[92] Gal 1:8

When the Church began to drift away from the Scripture as the sole guide for teaching and practice, it began to decline. Over time theology was formulated by councils of bishops, often consulting with monarchs rather than studying God's Word. Indeed, there came a time when access to the Scriptures was only afforded to the hierarchy, who rarely sought its counsel, and banned to the common man. This practice went on for many centuries until the Reformation and the printing press, made the Bible available to all. Today we not only have many different translations of Scripture, we also have access to the original writings, and powerful tools to help us read and understand. Thus, there is no excuse for ignorance of God's Word or will. Some would argue that all this access to Scripture has caused much division and doctrinal confusion. People having freedom to think for themselves always produces this. Nevertheless, the Scriptures were written for our instruction, and therefore if we are to know what God has said and is saying to us, we must be able to study them. This is also the reason God has given us teachers to open the Bible to us and help us understand what we are reading. We are not to get our theology from men, but from Scripture alone.

When I was a young man growing up in Catholic Ireland, I never had access to a Bible. We did not have one in our family, nor did I see one anywhere else. The Catholic hierarchy did not encourage the reading of the Bible, and indeed, for the most part, didn't read it themselves. There was a big one on the altar, with pictures of the popes laced throughout that had certain verses designated for the various services. Later, after Vatican II, they began to give us what they call "Misalettes" with prayers and little snippets of Bible passages. These I liked to read and I remember I had many questions. In those days, questions were not expected and there was little opportunity to ask. As I grew older however, I frequently felt that what the Church was teaching, and what the Bible was saying (the little bit I knew) were at odds. But when I did get the nerve to ask a priest, I was generally frustrated, because they had no answer. In fact, they seemed to dislike my asking that little Protestant word, "Why?" The standard answer to the difficult questions was always, "Holy Mother the Church says so." It is no surprise then that when I came to know the Lord in 1976 and got my own Bible, I read it over and over. Thank God for the Reformation! Thank God for the ability to read the Bible and digest its teaching these last 40 years. What a great opportunity God has given us. How horrible when the Bible was in the hands of the hierarchy alone and they were the only ones qualified to determine what God wanted us to think and do! You will understand then, why a statement such as this would cause me great concern:

"What is theology anyway? Here is my attempt at a definition: Theology is a human attempt to explain God's Word and God's works in a reasonable and systematic way. This is not a traditional definition. For one thing, it considers God's works as one valid source of theological information. For another, it sees God's Word as both what is written in the Bible (logos) as well as what God is currently revealing (rhea). Admittedly, a downside of viewing theology in this way is possible subjectivity, but the upside is more relevance to what the Spirit is currently saying to the churches on a practical level. Teachers research and expound the Logos, prophets bring the Rhema and apostles put it together and point the direction into the future."[93]

This small passage makes startling statements, all of which undermine Scripture as the sole authority for belief and practice. First, to say that theology is a human attempt to explain God's

---

[93]C. Peter Wagner, *Dominion!: How Kingdom Action Can Change the World* (Chosen Books, 2008), http://books.google.com/books?

Word and God's works is extremely misleading. Mr. Wagner admits this is not a traditional definition, but he continues with it regardless. However, the problem with this statement is that most believers think of theology and doctrine as one and the same. Therefore, to say that it is merely an "attempt" to explain God's Word is to suggest that one's theology may or may not be reliable. It could also suggest that we can't be certain of what God's Word says, since we are only attempting to know it. Then Mr. Wagner adds to this rather fluid definition the need to also understand "God's works," which appear to be something other than the Bible. Thus, what I perceive God to be doing or not doing, or speaking to me, is now as influential in formulating theology or doctrine as the Word of God. That's a shocker! But in case you think I'm exaggerating, he goes on to even redefine God's Word, saying it contains both what is written in the Bible, and what He is currently revealing -- as though there could be a difference. This is the old fallacy which says that the Greek word *logos* represents the written Word, and the word *rhema* represents what we hear God speaking to us. However, both are used interchangeably in the New Testament. Nevertheless, to suggest that what we believe God is speaking to us should be used to determine theology or doctrine is ludicrous. How do we know it is God speaking unless we examine it using the plumbline of the written Word?

Now I realize that God has not told us everything in the Bible. For instance, He has not told us who to marry, or where to go to church, or what profession we should or should not pursue. The Holy Spirit speaks to us and guides and directs our steps in all these matters. However, as we have already said, the sole authority for all doctrine and theology is Scripture. Theology is essentially the study of God, His character, nature, purpose, etc. Yet, none of this can be determined outside of the written Word of God. Therefore, to suggest that what we perceive God is speaking or revealing to us should be used alongside Scripture to determine theology, as though it carried the same weight, is to undermine the Bible. Mr. Wagner admits that formulating theology in this way lends itself to subjectivity, but he argues that it gives more "relevance to what the Spirit is saying to the churches on a practical level." Whatever that means, it is very clear that he, along with many others in the NAR, distinguish between what God has said and what He is now saying.

"I want to make it clear that my research methodology is not philosophical or theological (in the classical sense) nor exegetical or revelational, but rather phenomenological. I am not saying that any of these methodologies is right or wrong. Phenomenology clearly is not superior to exegesis. It is merely my personal choice. The phenomenological approach leads me to employ terms not found in the Bible, because I believe it is not necessary to only use the Word of God but to also combine the Word of God with accurate observations of the present-day works of God. I am not approaching this so much from the question of what God ought to do as much as what God is actually doing. What the Spirit has said to the churches is one thing, but what the Spirit is now saying to the churches is another."[94]

The idea that there is a difference between what God said to the Church in Scripture and what He is saying to the Church today is completely erroneous. In fact, the phrase, "What the Spirit is saying to the churches," comes from the last book of the Bible, where we are warned not to add or subtract. This is not to say that God is not speaking to prophets and churches today, but what He says will harmonize completely with Scripture. Also, if we are truly understanding what the Lord said

[94] C. Peter Wagner (2012-03-08). *Apostles Today* (p. 77). Baker Publishing Group.

to the New Testament Church, we will be hearing and understanding what He is saying to the Church today. The application may be slightly different, but the truth revealed will be the same. The Word spoken to them still applies to us and it is still what the Spirit is saying.

If it is a serious thing to elevate what we believe God is speaking to the Church today alongside Scripture, it would appear the NAR is prepared to go even further. In fact, the whole point of Mr. Wagner's new approach to theology was to suggest it should only be formulated by properly recognized and aligned apostles. He spells this out rather clearly when he says, *"Teachers research and expound the Logos (Bible), prophets bring the Rhema and apostles put it together."* Does this sound familiar? Where have we heard this before? The apostolic elite determine what God wants and the rest of us are to obey. I realize that some of you will think that this is a mistake. Mr. Wagner could not have said that. He could not have meant that teachers and prophets were unable to arrive at sound theology based on the Word of God alone. But that is precisely what he said. Furthermore, he is not alone in this assessment.

"I personally believe that in the 1990's and into the 21st century, as prophets and apostles are being restored back to proper order and function within the Church, many of these Church councils of leading present-truth ministers will be necessary. One particular apostle or prophet or camp will never receive the whole revelation for the establishing of prophets and apostles back into the Church. Many will have visions (even of Jesus), dreams, rhemas, angelic visitations and supernatural personal experiences and sovereign moves of the Holy Spirit in their meetings. But doctrines that claim to be binding on all Christians must not be established by only one apostle, prophet or camp. There must be meetings of a church council with other

leaders of past and present restorational streams of truth."[95]
(Emphasis Mine)

There you have it friend! No Christian, church or even "anointed apostle" can determine what is sound doctrine that is binding on all Christians. That will require councils of the apostolic elite. The Church hierarchy alone can make these determinations. So much for all the Bible study! It seems that understanding doctrine and theology is way too complicated for ordinary folks!

"Five Principles for Establishing Doctrine.
When the fivefold ministers come together to consider doctrines and practices this way, they will need to keep several areas of insight in mind: (1) the claimed revelation from God; (2) the fruit of the ministry among those who have received the doctrine or practice; (3) the supernatural working of God accompanying it; (4) the Logos and Rhema word of God application and authority for the doctrine or practice; and (5) the witness of the Spirit and the unified consent of those present."[96]

"One of the things that helped to keep the Early Church strong and healthy was their continual devotion to the apostles' doctrine (see Acts 2:42). However, you'll notice that there is no mention of a list of beliefs that the Bible declares to be the official record of important doctrines. It is safe to say the 'apostles' doctrine' is referring to something other than a specific list. Peter understood this when he exhorted the Church concerning 'present truth' (see 2 Peter 1:12). That phrase is to direct our attention to that which the Lord is emphasizing for this season. That is the apostle's doctrine. The word coming from apostles is to bring clarification of the Father's focus for the

_____

[95]Hamon, Bill. *Apostles Prophets and the Coming Moves of God: God's End-time Plans for His Church and Planet Earth*. Santa Rosa Beach, FL: Christian International, pg. 48
[96] Ibid

Church, and in turn strengthen our resolve to His purposes. Fresh revelation carries fresh fire, which helps us to maintain the much-needed fire in our souls. Apostles carry a blueprint in their hearts concerning the Church and God's purposes on the earth. They are used to bring fresh revelation to the Church. Apostolic teams are sent to represent their spiritual father, and carry the word that has been entrusted to their 'tribe.' They help bring an understanding and establish an order needed in the particular location they were sent to."[97]

In the above passage, Bill Johnson uses Acts 2:42 to equate the doctrine of the Twelve Apostles of the Lord with the teaching of apostles today. The Early Church was strong and healthy because they were devoted to the Apostles' teaching, he declares. Therefore, since NAR apostles are the apostles of today, if we want to be strong and healthy, we need to have the same devotion to their teaching (his included). What Bill is ignoring, however, is the context of the passage. As in Ephesians 2:20, it is *the* apostles and not just "apostles." It is the specific Apostles chosen by the Lord who were teaching the Scriptures (Old Testament) and unfolding the Messianic passages. Their teaching became Scripture and anyone who teaches God's people today, apostle or not, should bring the same teaching. In other words, the teaching of the apostles that we are to be devoted to is the Scripture itself. To use this verse regarding the teaching of today's apostles, is to put their revelations on the same level as Scripture.

Another point that is made by Bill in the passage above, is that the teaching of the apostles today is "present truth." He says

[97] Elijah List, Bill Johnson: *Apostolic Teams - a Group of People Who Carry the Family Mission -* Nov 21, 2008

the Apostles in Acts 2:42 did not have a specific list.[98] He then uses another passage is 2 Peter 1:12, to suggest they were teaching something called "present truth."

"Therefore, I will always be ready to remind you of these things, even though you already know them, and have been established in the truth which is present with you." 2 Pet 1:12 (Emphasis Mine)

How does the phrase, "the truth that is present with you" become "present truth?" The word is the same but the meaning is radically different. If you read the verse and the passage containing it, you will know that Peter is talking about the teaching of all the Apostles concerning the faith. This teaching is, of course, the teaching of Jesus and the revelation of Him in Scripture. Peter is not talking about some new revelation he had for the moment, but the faith once and for all delivered to the saints. It contained exhortations on how to walk with Christ in the present world, while waiting in hope of His coming. Indeed, that is the whole message of 2 Peter, with severe warnings against false teachers thrown in. He is merely telling the Church that they already have this teaching with them, and available to them -- "present with you." However, since he knows he is about to die, he is determined to write it down for them so that they will not forget. How then does one lift the idea of "present truth" out of this passage and suggest that it applies to new "revelations" being received by today's apostles? The answer is obvious. It can only happen to one who has taken heavy doses of the NAR Kool-Aid.

---

[98] Hebrews chapter 6 clearly presents a list of fundamental doctrines that were taught by the apostles!

Agenda-Driven Prophets

I have great respect for prophetic ministry. I have grown up in the Lord with it. I have a prophetic family and many good friends who are mature in the prophetic. And I can tell you that prophetic ministry, when it is functioning properly, is extremely comforting, encouraging and edifying. Some Christians have the idea that anyone who is a prophet must be perfect in what they speak and can't make a mistake. However, there is no need to discuss a comparison of Old and New Testament prophets, since Paul made it clear that prophetic words must be tested and judged and so must the ministry of folks who claim to be prophets.

"Let two or three prophets speak, and let the others pass judgment." 1Cor 14:29

The need for judgment to be made by the Church leaders implies that prophets can make mistakes. This is not to suggest that they should, but only that they can. As they mature in their knowledge of Christ and His Word, their words will be more reliable. Also, prophets are expected to bring what they believe God has spoken or revealed to them, and it is to be judged, meaning analyzed and discerned. Because a prophecy lines up with the teaching of Scripture does not necessarily make it true, but one cannot be outside of the teaching of Scripture and be speaking from God. Therefore, prophecy can never be put on a level with Scripture but must be always be judged by it. One who knows Scripture will immediately scan a prophecy, like an antivirus program, to see if it's healthy. This does not suggest a critical spirit, but rather a wise one. The same principle applies, of course, to all the teaching of the Word. It must also be scanned and judged by Scripture. And those whose hearts are right, and desire to build up the people of God, will welcome this process. Having laid that foundation, and acknowledging that there is wonderful prophetic ministry in the Church today, let us turn our attention to the Prophetic Movement which is controlled by the NAR.

True prophets in the Bible didn't speak lies, make up stuff, follow an agenda, or minister for hire. They simply spoke what God was saying, like it or not, and they were never popular. False prophets, on the other hand, were always numerous, prophesying from their own false visions, or the deception of their minds. They always spoke what was popular, and what the leaders wanted to hear.

"But, 'Ah, Lord GOD!' I said, 'Look, the prophets are telling them, 'You will not see the sword nor will you have famine, but I will give you lasting peace in this place.' Then the LORD said to me, 'The prophets are prophesying falsehood in My name. I have neither sent them nor commanded them nor spoken to them; they are prophesying to you a false vision, divination, futility and the deception of their own minds.'" Jer 14:13-14

To properly address the madness in the Prophetic Movement today would require much more space, and it would derail me from my current subject matter. So, let me just be frank and say the movement has gone amok, and is making a mess all over the Body of Christ. Rarely do they speak what God wants to say, but almost exclusively the agenda of the NAR. They bring forth the same old stuff over and over again, as they pass it from one to another, and pawn it off as new revelation. There will be a season of this and a season of that, the blessings of Joseph, windows of opportunity, special anointings, open heavens, new portals, and newer levels, and, of course, more breakthrough. Do they get it right occasionally? Of course, but when you fire a thousand bullets, something will surely be hit. Do I sound a bit cynical? Perhaps I am, but it's only because I am grieved at how they mislead God's people with the full knowledge and support of the apostles. And their revelations from their visits to heaven are placed on the same par with the Word of God, as they fly around decreeing them over the earth. I wish I were lying, but unfortunately, I am telling the truth. These individuals feel that they are authorized to make these prophetic decrees based on what they believe God wants to do, rather than simply hearing what God is saying.

"Making A Kingdom Decree teaches you that God has given you the power to decree a heavenly thing on earth and it would be established for you! When a decree is made on earth, it begins to take root and build a foundation to establish the kingdom of God!"[99]

"We need the prophets to announce, decree, impart and activate. But in this hour, we need prophets who pray more than we need prophets who predict. We need prophets who trumpet a message of repentance more than we need prophets who are experts at pronouncing judgment. We need prophets of awakening who will speak to the roots of revival in our nation and command them to rise again more than we need prophets who curse the land."[100]

This is a word written to the "doom and gloom" prophets (I suppose I'm one of those) by Jennifer LeClaire. It is typical of the attitude of the NAR toward prophets and prophecy. The prophets are to follow the agenda and do what the apostles say. They are to serve the apostles like the magicians and sorcerers in ancient Egypt or Chaldea served the king. Like Merlins in the king's court, they prophesy the Kingdom decrees and use their

---

[99] *Making A Kingdom Decree* (teaching CD) by Jeremy Lopez
[100] *When Prophets of Doom Predict Natural Disasters on Specific Dates That Don't Come to Pass*, Jennifer LeClaire, *Charisma Magazine*, 10/28/2015

powers to guarantee success. Are these the prophets we need in the Church today? Certainly not! We need prophets who read the Bible, spend time with God, hear what the Holy Spirit is saying, and proclaim it boldly, even if it's unpopular.

"'Therefore behold, I am against the prophets,' declares the LORD, 'who steal My words from each other. Behold, I am against the prophets,' declares the LORD, 'who use their tongues and declare, "The Lord declares." 'Behold, I am against those who have prophesied false dreams,' declares the LORD, 'and related them and led My people astray by their falsehoods and reckless boasting; yet I did not send them or command them, nor do they furnish this people the slightest benefit,' declares the LORD.'" Jer 23:30-32

With all the craziness in the Church today, don't you wish you could talk to the early apostles and get their take on it? What about an afternoon with the Apostle Paul, where we could ask him any question about the Bible we didn't understand? Wouldn't that be cool? I know we have his epistles, but they are so misinterpreted that it is hard to know what to believe sometimes. Well, I have good news and bad news. In his book *The Final Quest*, Rick Joyner reveals how he was in heaven and had a discussion with the Apostle Paul, and the great apostle seemed a bit discouraged. I do acknowledge that this is on the loony side of things, but to this date, no one has taken Mr. Joyner to the woodshed. Instead, these writings earned him great stature.

"I then felt compelled to look at those who were sitting on the thrones we were passing. As I did, my gaze fell upon a man whom I knew was the apostle Paul. As I looked back at the Lord, He motioned for me to speak to him. I have so looked forward to this I said, feeling awkward but excited by this meeting. (RICK)

'I know that you are aware of just how much your letters have guided the Church, and they are probably still accomplishing more than all the rest of us put together. You are still one of the greatest lights on the earth.' (PAUL) 'Thank you,' he said graciously. 'But you do not understand just how much we have looked forward to meeting you. You are a soldier in the last battle; you are the ones whom everyone here is waiting to meet. We only saw these days dimly through our limited prophetic vision, but you have been chosen to live in them. You are a soldier preparing for the last battle. You are the ones for whom we are all waiting.' (RICK) Still feeling awkward, I continued, 'But there is no way that I can convey the appreciation that we feel for you, and all who helped to set our course with their lives and their writings. I also know that we will have an eternity for exchanging our appreciation, so please, while I am here, let me ask, "What would you say to my generation that will help us in this battle?"' (PAUL) 'I can only say to you now what I have already said to you through my writings. I would have you to understand them better by knowing that I fell short of all that I was called to do,' Paul stated, looking me resolutely in the eyes. (RICK) 'But you are here, in one of the greatest thrones. You are still reaping more fruit for eternal life than any of us could ever hope to reap,' I protested. (PAUL) 'By the grace of God I was able to finish my course, but I still did not walk in all that I was called to. I fell short of the highest purposes that I could have walked in. Everyone has. I know that some think that is blasphemy to think of me as anything less than the greatest example of Christian ministry, but I was being honest when I wrote near the end of my life that I was the greatest of sinners. I was not saying that I have been the greatest of sinners, but that I was the greatest of sinners then. I had been given so much to understand, and I walked in so little of it.'[101] (Emphasis Mine)

---

[101] The Final Quest, Rick Joyner, Morning Star Publications, 1996, pp. 131-132.

As bad as this is, there is much more in this so-called revelation that is even worse. Wherever Mr. Joyner was, I can assure you it was not heaven. That's the good news. Regardless, I include it here to illustrate the folly of placing prophetic revelation alongside Scripture, as the NAR apostles advocate. If this kind of thing is presented with Paul's writings in Scripture, must we depend on the "apostles" to "put it together" for us? Mr. Joyner contradicts the Scriptures in the above press conference he had with Paul, when he "quotes" the apostle as saying that he "fell short of the highest purposes he could have walked in." Let me guess, was that "social transformation?" Also, Joyner has Paul saying that he was literally the greatest of sinners at the time he was writing Scripture. Are you serious? So now that Paul has spoken again, according to Joyner, and contradicted himself, we have a problem. I guess the following verses were a mistake!

"I have fought the good fight, I have finished the course, I have kept the faith; in the future there is laid up for me the crown of righteousness, which the Lord, the righteous Judge, will award to me on that day; and not only to me, but also to all who have loved His appearing." 2 Tim 4:7-8

While setting the stage for the revealing of his trance experiences, Mr. Joyner gives five levels of prophetic revelation. Look what he places on the third level:

"The next level of revelation is conscious sense of the presence of the Lord, or the anointing of the Holy Spirit, which gives special illumination to our minds. This often comes when I am writing, or speaking, and it gives me much greater confidence in the importance or accuracy of what I am saying. I believe that this was probably experienced by the apostles as they wrote the New Testament epistles. This will give us great confidence, but

it is still a level where we can still be influenced by our prejudices, doctrines, etc. This is why I believe, in certain matters, Paul would say that he was giving his opinion, but that he thought he had [the agreement of] the Spirit of the Lord. ..."[102]

Wow! Did you get that? The Apostles were operating in lower levels of revelation when they wrote the Scriptures, where they were still being influenced by their prejudices, doctrines, etc. In other words, there was the potential for mistakes. He suggests that this is why Paul said, "he was giving his opinion." Of course, he is dead wrong; Paul only said that in 1 Corinthians 7, regarding marriage, because Jesus had not specifically addressed the issue he was referring to.[103] But when Joyner wrote *The Final Quest* while he was in a trance, he was operating in a higher level of revelation, where there is less room for error. This is clearly planting doubts about the reliability of the written Word, and suggesting that his revelations may be purer.

Conclusion

For centuries, Christians were denied the opportunity to read the Scriptures. Many were executed for trying to translate them. The Catholic hierarchy maintained that the Bible was too deep for the "laity" to interpret. Of course, they were afraid that people would find out the truth. Thanks to men like John Huss, William Tyndale, John Wycliffe, and, of course, Martin Luther, the people of God were given a Bible to read, and the faith was passed down to all of us. Now, these apostles and prophets of the NAR want the Church to return to the thinking of the Middle Ages and believe that only they, and their appointed councils, can interpret what God is saying and doing. Give me a break! Furthermore, they want to impose on us the notion that their

---

[102] *The Final Quest*, Rick Joyner, Morning Star Publications, 1996, p.9
[103] 1 Cor 7:10,12,40

revelations and spiritual experiences, no matter how bizarre, should be laid next to the Bible to determine the will of God. They call this "present truth" or "new light." However, by doing this, they undermine the Word of God, and make themselves no better than the Jehovah's Witnesses with their "new light," or the Mormons with their phony, occultic additions to the Bible. Friends, it is time to speak up. Loving Jesus, embracing revival, and walking in Father's love, does not mean we must be silent while the truth is maligned. On the contrary, we must preach the Word, in season and out,[104] whether popular or not, always knowing that the Word of God cannot be imprisoned![105]

---

[104] 2 Tim 4:2
[105] 2 Tim 2:9

Chapter Six
Ours is The Dominion?

The development of the concept of "present truth" was essential to the agenda of the NAR apostles. They must place their current revelation, which radically departs from that of the Twelve, on a level with Scripture for it to be taken seriously. They will all argue, of course, that this was the work of the Holy Spirit and not any human plan, and they are genuine in that belief. Nevertheless, we have already seen that these teachings came from the founders of the movement and have become the standard playbook. Originally, the term "present truth" was used of "restored truth" -- truth that was contained in Scripture and taught by the Early Church, but lost to subsequent generations. But over time, however, "present truth" came to be viewed as that which the Holy Spirit is saying to the Church today, regardless of the understanding of the New Testament Church. This view, as we have seen, was articulated by the father of the NAR, C.P. Wagner, and was disseminated throughout the movement. It is unclear if all the apostles and prophets understand the teaching, but it doesn't seem to matter. Aligning with Scripture has taken a back seat to aligning with the new apostles and their sacred agenda. What is this agenda, you may ask? What is this "present truth" being emphasized by the Holy Spirit? It is social transformation.

"The Holy Spirit is now speaking to the churches and saying that God's people must do what it takes to transform society, segment by segment, until God's kingdom is seen on earth as it is in heaven."[106]

---

[106] C. Peter Wagner, *"Transform Society!"* Global Prayer News, Vol. 6, No. 3, Jul-Sep 2000

"Social transformation, as I have been saying, is one of the strongest words that the Holy Spirit is clearly speaking to the churches today."[107]

The mission of the Church, according to Wagner, is to transform society. Social transformation is now the mandate for every believer. Indeed, we must all do whatever it takes to get it done. This mantra now permeates the NAR, regardless of their eschatological[108]viewpoint. That, together with the desire to be recognized apostles and prophets, seems to be the enticement for alignment. And once alignment has been achieved, theology becomes secondary.

When we analyze this new social gospel, we realize that it is not taught anywhere in the New Testament. Where in the words of Jesus or the writers of the New Testament (unless we twist them as the NAR does), will we find the call to go out and transform society socially? It is not there! And the proof that it is not there is not only in the text, it is evidenced by the lives of the Apostles and the Early Church fathers. Mr. Wagner knew this, of course, but he avoided it by suggesting they were unable to do it.

"To trace this back, the beginning centuries of Christianity were a time of severe persecution. For the most part, believers did not have the power to transform the society of the Roman Empire, where most of them found themselves."[109]

This is a most disturbing and condescending statement. The Early Church didn't have the power? Really? The 1st Century Church was filled with the power of God and they spread the

---

[107] *The Church in the Workplace: How God's People Can Transform Society*, by C. Peter Wagner, pg. 34, Regal Books
[108] Eschatology is the study of End-Times.
[109] *The Church in the Workplace: How God's People Can Transform Society*, by C. P. Wagner, pg. 38, Regal Books

gospel, given to them by Jesus (the gospel of the Kingdom), all over the Roman Empire. They did not preach a gospel of social transformation because that is not the gospel of Christ. If it had been, they would have preached it and would have transformed the Roman Empire. What they preached was repentance and faith in Messiah, and the reality of His Kingdom that is coming. They were told to bring this gospel to all the nations and then the end would come.[110] The end, of course brings the Tribulation period and the Return of Christ.[111] But to Mr. Wagner and a growing number of the NAR apostles who are Preterists,[112] the end came in 70AD.

"Jesus answered, 'My kingdom is not of this world. If My kingdom were of this world, then My servants would be fighting so that I would not be handed over to the Jews; but as it is, My kingdom is not of this realm.'" John 18:36 (Emphasis Mine)

Jesus did not preach a political message, nor did He involve Himself in the affairs of the Roman Empire. He said His Kingdom was not of this world. His disciples never took over a city, a town, or even a village, and they certainly would have if they thought they had that mandate. Neither did they advocate doing this. They did not tell their followers to infiltrate worldly systems, or governments, or the so-called 7 Mountains of Culture, because they understood the Kingdom was not of this world. They carried out their commission, which was to make disciples of Jews and Gentiles, and to teach them all that Jesus commanded. They knew the kingdom was to come when He returned, even though they had received a foretaste of that future glory.[113] To suggest otherwise is to distort their record,

---

[110] Mt 24:14

[111] Mt 24:15 follows Mt 24:14 because it is the end spoken of.

[112] Preterists believe that all the prophecies regarding the end of the age were fulfilled in 70 AD or thereabouts. Thus, the end-times are over. Please see Appendix A

[113] Rom 8:23, Eph 1:14, Heb 6:5

make them ignorant of Scripture and disobedient to God. Yet that is exactly what the NAR and its host of apostles do, by their insistence on social transformation and 7 Mountains Dominion.

"This is the government of the Church of the future that will arise and spread My light throughout the world in the latter days. This government will overcome all other governments. When this is in order, you can then command the governments of the earth to come into order."[114]

"The first advent of Christ was for the purpose of creating a blessed seed upon the earth -- the Church. The second coming of Jesus will take place after this blessed seed has completed the Dominion Process upon the earth by making disciples of all nations."[115]

"We all agree that the society to be transformed is not just one big conglomerate, but a unified whole that is made up of several vital pieces, each one of which must take its own path toward transformation. These segments of society should be seen as apostolic spheres."[116]

"Dominion theology is predicated upon three basic beliefs: 1) satan usurped man's dominion over the earth through the temptation of Adam and Eve; 2) The Church is God's instrument to take dominion back from satan; 3) Jesus cannot or will not return until the Church has taken dominion by gaining control of the earth's governmental and social institutions."[117]

---

[114] Chuck Pierce, *The Future War of the Church: How We Can Defeat Lawlessness and Bring God's Order to the Earth*, Regal Books, 2001, pages 31-32

[115] Mark Pfeifer, *Theology of Reclaiming 7 Mountains: The Dominion Process,"* http://www.reclaim7mountains.com/apps/articles/default.asp?articleid=41538&columnid=4347

[116] C. Peter Wagner, *The Church in the Workplace*, (Regal, 2006), p. 112.

[117] Al Dager, *Vengeance Is Ours: The Church In Dominion*

"Kris sounds a clear prophetic call to embrace change. Throughout the pages of this book he commissions us to make earth like heaven. You will receive an impartation of supernatural faith and courage as you journey through the pages of this book and become part of the kingdom mandate to transform society." [118]

"The coming Elijah Revolution will affect the entire world and will prepare the way of the Lord before His return. According to Scripture, Jesus will sit at God's right hand until all of His enemies are put under His feet. The Elijah Revolution will accomplish this as God's end-time emissaries confront seven nations 'greater and mightier than we' -- the Hittites, Girgashites, Amorites, Canaanites, Perizzites, Hivites, and Jebusites. These nations correspond to seven 'mountains' of global society -- Media, Government, Education, Economy, Religion, Celebration/Arts, and Family…. With divine power and favor, revolutionaries will take these mountains for Christ! If you want to do your part, come now and be trained and equipped." [119]

"As fanatical as it may sound to fundamental evangelical Christians, the Church is destined to subdue all things and put all things under Christ's feet before He literally returns from heaven. Father God said to Jesus, "Sit thou at my right hand until I make all your enemies your footstool…." [120]

The above quotes are only a tiny sample of the writings of the NAR that are becoming mainstream in the Church today. As you

---

[118] Endorsement by Ché Ahn, Apostle, Harvest Apostolic Center, of the book, *"How Heaven Invades Earth, Transform the World Around You"* by Kris Vallotton
[119] *The Seven Mountain Prophecy: Unveiling the Coming Elijah Revolution* by Johnny Enlow, Creation House
[120] Quote attributed to Bill Hamon, Bill Hamon, "Dr. Bill Hamon answers your questions about the eternal Church," interview with Jennifer LeClaire

can see, the focus is clearly on society and culture. With few exceptions, they seem convinced that the Church must take over the world and reign before Jesus comes. This is their understanding of the Great Commission – to transform society. And to back up their wild statements and visions, they quote two or three Bible verses that have been doctored to the cause, or that belong to the period known as the Millennium, when Christ Himself will rule from Jerusalem. The following is an example of this:

"The LORD says to my Lord: 'Sit at My right hand until I make Your enemies a footstool for Your feet.'" Psalm 110:1

This verse portrays Jesus sitting at the right hand of the Father until His enemies are defeated. Therefore, it is easy to deduct that the Church must execute His dominion over the earth in this age, since He Himself is in heaven. However, the verse must be put together with the rest of Scripture on the topic. Many Scriptures tell us most of this will be fulfilled during the Tribulation period by the direct and literal intervention of Christ. Yet, Paul makes it clear that it is not completed until after the Millennial Reign, when the last enemy to be done away with is death.

"But each in his own order: Christ the first fruits, after that those who are Christ's at His coming, then comes the end, when He hands over the kingdom to the God and Father, when He has abolished all rule and all authority and power. For He must reign until He has put all His enemies under His feet. The last enemy that will be abolished is death. For HE HAS PUT ALL THINGS IN SUBJECTION UNDER HIS FEET. But when He says, 'All things are put in subjection,' it is evident that He is excepted who put all things in subjection to Him. When all things are subjected to Him, then the Son Himself also will be subjected to the One who

subjected all things to Him, so that God may be all in all." 1 Cor 15:23-28

The context of this Scripture is the Millennial Reign when Christ will rule the earth and destroy all His enemies. The last enemy to be removed is death. Then we are told that He will hand over the Kingdom to God the Father. Thus, since death clearly exists in the Millennium period,[121] and is not abolished until the end of it, the destruction of Christ's enemies is accomplished by Christ Himself when He comes to rule and reign. It is likely that Psalm 110:1 refers to this age, when Christ sits at God's right hand and watches the Father bring all His enemies against Israel, where He pours out His wrath on them and rules for a thousand years.

I realize, of course, that Preterists believe we are already in the Millennium, or that the church will establish it in this age. Nevertheless, they must account for the fact that things on planet earth are not getting better as they say. Christ has more enemies than ever, and sin and death continue to increase. Therefore, if they are going to conquer all Jesus' enemies, they must make every person His voluntary disciple (including those who hate Him and reject Him) and abolish death by making all flesh immortal. No small feat, but the great apostles seem undaunted by the challenge.

Eschatology Determines Behavior

"What we think about the end has everything to do with how we behave in the middle. So we must align our thinking regarding our end times beliefs with truth, so that our behavior in the now is that of responsibility and hope."[122]

---

[121] Isaiah 65:20, Rev 20:9

[122] *Is It the End of The World as We Know It?* by Kris Vallotton, December 5, 2016
http://krisvallotton.com/is-it-the-end-of-the-world-as-we-know-it

The above quote is from someone who appears to espouse Preterist Theology (that the End-Times ended in the 1st Century and the world is getting better and better), yet his conclusion is what I have been saying for a long time. Eschatology matters. Indeed, our view of the End-Times determines how we live and how we prepare for the future. It would also seem that it will determine what happens to us in the future. Let us consider for a moment then, the primary End-Time worldviews that exist today. This will require a little history.

Throughout the 20th Century, the church in revival and restoration was almost exclusively Pre-Millennial. Pre-Millennialism is the view that the end of the age and the Tribulation are future, followed by the visible return of Christ and the Millennium. This view is clearly taught in Scripture, and a straightforward, literal reading of the Bible leads to no other conclusion. This was the view of the Hebrew Prophets as they proclaimed the coming Day of the Lord, and the Apostles of Christ, who made it clear that they waited for Messiah's coming to rescue the godly[123] and bring in everlasting righteousness -- His Kingdom in Jerusalem. This was also the view of the Church throughout the 1st and 2nd Centuries. However, in the 3rd Century some began to arise preaching Amillennialism,[124] such as the heretical Origen, and it was later codified in the 4th Century by the writings of Augustine. Both men were heavily influenced by anti-Semitism (Replacement Theology)[125] and Gnostic Dualism.[126]

---

[123] 1Thess 1:10

[124] Amillennialism rejects the idea of a literal 1000-year physical reign of Christ on the earth, and believes that since the Ascension we have been in the Millennial Reign otherwise known as the "Church Age."

[125] Replacement Theology is the belief that Israel was rejected by God and all her promises were given to the Church who replaced her - the good ones, that is.

[126] Essentially the idea of two equal opposing forces, light and darkness, good and evil, spiritual and physical. For instance, many Gnostics considered the material world as evil and therefore

Amillennialism was the primary eschatological view throughout the Dark Ages until the Reformation, when a view known as Historicism[127] was crafted. The Preterist view was compiled by a Jesuit priest[128] during the Counter Reformation, to combat the claims of the Protestants who believed the Pope was the Antichrist. Though some believe that Calvin was a Preterist, this approach to Biblical prophecy never caught on among Protestants, although it was kept alive and massaged in their ranks. Then in the late 20th Century it underwent a revival among Evangelicals with the teaching of Rousas J. Rushdoony. This created a stir for a while, and found inroads in the homeschool movement, but was soundly rejected by Evangelical and Charismatic leaders alike. The restoration of the church, Israel, and sound Biblical eschatology, during the sixties, seventies, and eighties, left no room for a return to such medieval drivel. This was a time when the Body of Christ had real teachers and scholars (such as Derek Prince), who were not afraid to teach and warn the church against false teaching. Nevertheless, by the late eighties and early nineties, many began to unwisely de-emphasize theology in favor of unity. Nowhere was this more prevalent, than in eschatology. The primary disagreements of the time were concerning the timing of the Rapture (Pre-Tribulation or Pre-Trib, Mid-Tribulation or Mid-Trib and Post-Tribulation or Post-Trib). This led many pastors and leaders to conclude that the teaching of eschatology was unimportant, and they began to ignore it altogether, suggesting they were "Pan-Trib," since it would all "pan out." Some continue with this stupid expression of ignorance, seemingly unaware of what's

---

had no place for a literal Kingdom. The most extreme form of this was Manichaean Gnosticism. Prior to his conversion to Christianity, Augustine was a Manichaean.

[127] The Historicist view is that Biblical prophecy is being fulfilled in a progressive manner, throughout history, rather than in one generation.

[128] Jesuit Luis de Alcasar (1554–1613) wrote the first systematic preterist exposition of prophecy - *Vestigatio arcani sensus in Apocalypsi* (published in 1614) - during the Counter-Reformation. The word "Preterism" is derived from the Latin "Praeter" meaning "past."

going on around them. Into this vacuum of sound theology, or rejection of sound theology, came the repackaged and refurbished Dominionism and Preterism of C.P. Wagner.

Sitting Ducks for Deception

Because of the disdain of Charismatic and Revival leaders for sound eschatology, and their "it will all pan out" attitude, in a sense it did pan out. Because of their ignorance and confusion, they became sitting ducks for deception. Mr. Wagner himself seems to have wandered down this path. In his book, *This Changes Everything: How God Can Transform Your Mind and Change Your Life*, he details his "conversion" to Preterism.

"Remember most of my career as a Christian leader, I held the futurist view. It carries some very positive aspects, not the least of which is the urgent call for evangelism and world missions. The unprecedented surge of the missionary movement during the twentieth century and the explosive growth of world Christianity was significantly fueled by futurists. For example, the Pentecostal movement turned out to be the strongest driving force for world missions during the last century, and virtually all Pentecostals would be what theologians would call eschatological futurists. Eschatological futurists view all the end-time prophecies in the future tense, and I was one of them. With all this, then, why change a paradigm."[129]

It is one thing to have come from a Preterist tradition and known nothing else. However, it is quite another thing to understand the clear teachings of the Bible about the end of the age and the soon return of Christ, and then to discard it. Nevertheless, I want to point out that Mr. Wagner admits the best evangelists and missionaries, who caused the explosive growth of

---

[129] *"This Changes Everything: How God Can Transform Your Mind and Change Your Life."* C.P. Wagner, 2013, Chosen Books

Christianity throughout the 20th century, were not Preterists, but Futurists. Of course they were! This is always the case, because Futurists who are eagerly awaiting the return of Christ are concerned with souls and not systems. Furthermore, if the "apostles" were about transformation of culture, they would be all about evangelism, instead of trying to take over the 7 Mountains, since this is the only way culture ever changes. In any event, Wagner continues with the explanation of his transformation:

"Well, the bible says that we know in part. In other words, nobody knows everything, and I believe that this applies especially to the field of eschatology. Good people have good biblical and practical reasons for holding each one of the three main views: futurist, preterist and partial preterist. I will soon explain why I switched from futurist to partial preterist.... The full preterist view believes that all the end-time prophecies of the Bible have already been fulfilled, including the marriage feast of the Lamb, Jesus' appearance on a white horse, the resurrection of the dead, the separation of the sheep and goat nations, the new heaven and the new earth, and several other things that seem to others like they still belong in the future. Partial preterists agree that much end-time prophecy, has, indeed, been fulfilled, but that some things, including those that I just mentioned, are still in the future. I do not believe that I need to give details as to why I disagree with full preterism, but I will mention that my good friend John Eckhardt espouses this position, and explains it quite thoroughly in his book, Come Quickly, Lord Jesus."[130]

Did you get that? "Good people have good Biblical and practical reasons for holding each of the three main views."

---

[130] *This Changes Everything: How God Can Transform Your Mind and Change Your Life.* CP Wagner, 2013, Chosen Books

Really? They have "Biblical" reasons for holding onto Full Preterism? This is outrageous! Virtually all Bible scholars consider Full Preterism heresy, as do the Partial Preterists. The Bible certainly does. They deny any return of Christ, and claim that both resurrections have already taken place.

"Be diligent to present yourself approved to God as a workman who does not need to be ashamed, accurately handling the word of truth. But avoid worldly and empty chatter, for it will lead to further ungodliness, and their talk will spread like gangrene. Among them are Hymenaeus and Philetus, men who have gone astray from the truth saying that the resurrection has already taken place, and they upset the faith of some. Nevertheless, the firm foundation of God stands, having this seal, 'The Lord knows those who are His,' and, 'Everyone who names the name of the Lord is to abstain from wickedness."' 2 Tim 2:15-19 (Emphasis Mine)

It's alarming how casually Wagner explains Full Preterist beliefs; that Jesus has already come on a white horse, the marriage supper has taken place, the Resurrection has already happened, the nations have been judged, and we are in the new heavens and the new earth. Then he points out that he disagreed, and the few who know what this means give a sigh of relief. But wait a minute. He condoned Full Preterists as having "Biblical reasons," and put their views on a par with Futurism. And though he tried to distance himself from it, he didn't succeed, since he said that his "good friend" John Eckhardt believes it and has written a book on it. Why was he good friends with a heretic? Obviously, he didn't believe Full Preterism was heresy. John Eckhardt is a big name in the NAR as we have already seen, yet to my knowledge, no one has come out confronting his Full Preterist views. Could it be that they are unfamiliar with his views, despite his writings, and Wagner's writings about him? I wonder how many other Full Preterists there are in the Apostolic Movement? But as we have seen, alignment trumps theology.

Now, let's finish the story of how Peter Wagner abandoned sound Biblical theology for Preterism.

"Things first began to change, however, when I became involved in spiritual warfare back in the 1990s, as I related in chapter 7, 'From Tolerating satan to a Declaration of War.' Instead of just sitting back and allowing satan to have free reign, in promoting his schemes of wickedness and injustice, I learned that God had provided powerful weapons of spiritual warfare that he expected us to use against the principalities of darkness, to help neutralize the enemy's evil advances. As we moved out, we discovered, that if we used these weapons broadly enough and effectively enough, whole previously unreached people groups could break satan's stranglehold and receive messengers of the gospel or the good news. This planted some doubts in my mind as to whether the world was supposed to get worse and worse in preparation for the rapture. These doubts escalated significantly around the turn of the century, give or take a couple of years on both sides. That is when I began adopting many of the new paradigms that I have been discussing, such as the kingdom of God, the church in the workplace and transforming society. One after the other had as its driving force a vision for the world to get better and better, not worse and worse." [131] *Emphasis Mine*

This is a sad story, but I wanted to use it to illustrate how a man of God became confused about Scripture and what he believed because he did not possess what he knew. This is the state of many Charismatics and Revival people, who generally think it's

---

[131] *This Changes Everything: How God Can Transform Your Mind and Change Your Life.* CP Wagner, 2013, Chosen Books

wonderful when a preacher gets a "new revelation." But this revelation was not from God. "How can you say that?" some of you will ask. "Are you saying that your eschatology is the only right one?"

This exact charge was leveled at me several years ago by a leader in the Revival Movement. I must admit I was startled at the time and didn't have a good comeback. The fact is that Preterism and Partial Preterism are not different views of eschatology. They are not eschatology -- period. They are not different views of the End-Times, because there are no End-Times for the Preterist, since the prophecies were all fulfilled two thousand years ago. Nevertheless, what is most troubling about this story is that doubts came into his mind while he was engaged in spiritual warfare. Without getting into the whole area of literally wrestling with principalities, something that is dangerous and seems to be spoken against in Scripture,[132] it is curious where these doubts came from. Nowhere in the Bible is there a hint that the world will get better and better before the literal return of Christ. In fact, it is the opposite. Jesus said that both the wheat and the tares would grow together and Christians and Jews would be hated by all nations. He even queried whether He would find the faith on the earth when He came. Mr. Wagner knew these passages, but suddenly, because of a perceived breakthrough against satan, he began to think things don't have to get worse and worse. Who really lost that battle? What got into his head to stop focusing on winning souls and start teaching Christians that things will get better and better? And the irony of all this is that Partial Preterism, which he was about to embrace, believes that satan and his angelic principalities were thrown down to earth in 70AD, or bound since then, depending on who you speak to. So much for all the

---

[132] 2 Pet 2:10, Jude 1:8

binding and pulling down of strongholds.

In 2006, Mr. Wagner states that he was given a book by Harold Eberle (another Preterist friend of his), which convinced him he was a Preterist. What is sad is that he never mentions going back to reading the Bible or seeking God through prayer, but merely his doubts, a new book and a new message -- victorious eschatology.

Is Partial Preterism Heresy?
We have discussed Full Preterism already and concluded that it is clearly heresy. Indeed, Partial Preterists, by and large, are adamant that Full Preterism is heresy. But what about Partial Preterism? Is it heresy? Before you start thinking about all the great people that believe it, and how terrible it is to call someone with a "different point of view" a heretic, let me say what I think it is, and then you can decide. Partial Preterism is false teaching and dangerous deception. Now that's better than heresy -- right?

Partial Preterism teaches that all the predictions of the Hebrew prophets, the teaching of Jesus (Matthew 24-25, Mark13, Luke 17 & 21), and the Book of Revelation, except for the last couple of chapters, were fulfilled in 70AD, and later with the fall of Rome. Think about this! They believe these verses, Matthew 24:29-31, took place in 70AD with the destruction of Jerusalem.

"But immediately after the tribulation of those days THE SUN WILL BE DARKENED, AND THE MOON WILL NOT GIVE ITS LIGHT, AND THE STARS WILL FALL from the sky, and the powers of the heavens will be shaken. And then the sign of the Son of Man will appear in the sky, and then all the tribes of the earth will mourn, and they will see the SON OF MAN COMING ON THE CLOUDS OF THE SKY with power and great glory. And

*He will send forth His angels with A GREAT TRUMPET and THEY
WILL GATHER TOGETHER His elect from the four winds, from
one end of the sky to the other." Mt 24:29-31*

Honestly! Did the sun and the moon not give light for an
extended time in 70AD? No! Did stars or asteroids fall from the
sky and impact the earth? No! Were men fainting from fear at
the roaring of the sea and the waves?[133] No! Were the powers
of the heavens shaken? No! Was Jesus seen by all the tribes of
the earth who were mourning for Him? No! No! No! How then
can they get away with this? Well, it's easy. They just say the
imagery was all symbolic and figurative and not to be taken
literally. Jesus came in judgment of Jerusalem and the Jews and
that was the last days of the Old Covenant.

*"Victorious eschatology makes a convincing argument that the
Biblical prophecies concerning the "last days" or the "end
times" were literally fulfilled at the time of the destruction of
Jerusalem in 70 A.D. The end times marked the ending of the
old covenant and the beginning of the new covenant. Jesus
literally will return to the earth in the future (see Matthew 24:36-
25:46), but none of the signs of Matthew 24:4-34 are expected
to precede His return, because they have already occurred. This
is known by professional theologians as the Partial Preterist view
of eschatology, and it is the view with which I personally
identify."[134]*

It seems that Partial Preterists, also known as Moderate
Preterists, massaged Preterism to make it a bit more believable
and so that they could squeeze into the creeds of the Church,
which were written much later than 70AD. These creeds clearly
state that Jesus is coming back again to judge the living and the

---

[133] Luke 21:25-26
[134] C. Peter Wagner, *Dominion!: How Kingdom Action Can Change the World*, p. 61-62

dead. Therefore, they say there is another Second Coming, when the Resurrection takes place and the saints are gathered. But there is no Antichrist, no Tribulation, no Armageddon or judgment of the nations, left to go. What Beast and False Prophet are then bound in Revelation chapter 19, and why is the Messiah coming through the clouds and fulfilling Ezekiel 38 & 39?

Partial Preterists are also either Amillennialists[135] or Post-Millennialists.[136] They believe that the gospel must be preached to all the nations during this period, which again illustrates the utter confusion of their thinking. Jesus said in Matthew 24:14 that the gospel must be preached to all the nations for a witness, and then the end of the age would come. In the next verse, He gave the sign of the end as the Abomination of Desolation. Since they believe that all this happened in 70AD, why are we still preaching the gospel? And why is the wolf not laying with the lamb[137] and why is there still warfare?[138]

The Two Pillars of Errant Eschatology
Preterism contradicts Scripture and history in so many ways that I cannot address in this chapter.[139] However, I will address the two main pillars that Preterism, and all the other views other than Premillennialism, are built upon. Please bear in mind that Postmillennialism and Dominion Theology (or Kingdom Now Theology) are, for the most part, one and the same.

---

[135] For Amillennialists there is no Millennium. Jesus is ruling and reigning spiritually from heaven since 70AD.
[136] Post-Millennialists believe the Church must bring the Kingdom or Millennium to the world before Jesus can come again.
[137] Isaiah 65:25
[138] Isaiah 2:4
[139] For more on the error of Preterism see Appendix A

1. Replacement Theology

There are many references in the writings of the Hebrew prophets regarding the destruction and scattering of Israel and her regathering from the ends of the earth at the end of the age. The Preterists consider these verses to have been fulfilled in the return from Babylon when only a small number of Jews returned. They also consider the Last Days to have ended in 70 AD, which was the period of the destruction of Israel and not a regathering from all the nations. The Prophets were very specific when they prophesied the final return, making it clear that Israel would be surrounded by all nations; but this last time, God would fight for them and they would be victorious (Micah 4:11-13, Isaiah 41:8-16). But even if we accept the view that this was fulfilled by the return from Babylon, as the Preterists say, what are we to do with Zechariah who prophesied after the return from Babylon? He said that all the nations would come against Israel and Jerusalem to destroy it, but the Jews would be victorious when God fights for them. When was this prophecy fulfilled? When did all the nations come against Jerusalem and when were they destroyed? Certainly not in 70 AD!

"'On that day, when all the nations of the earth are gathered against her, I will make Jerusalem an immovable rock for all the nations. All who try to move it will injure themselves. On that day I will strike every horse with panic and its rider with madness,' declares the LORD. 'I will keep a watchful eye over the house of Judah, but I will blind all the horses of the nations. Then the leaders of Judah will say in their hearts, "The people of Jerusalem are strong, because the LORD Almighty is their God." On that day I will make the leaders of Judah like a firepot in a woodpile, like a flaming torch among sheaves. They will consume right and left all the surrounding peoples, but Jerusalem will remain intact in her place. The LORD will save the dwellings of Judah first, so that the honor of the house of David

and of Jerusalem's inhabitants may not be greater than that of Judah. On that day the LORD will shield those who live in Jerusalem, so that the feeblest among them will be like David, and the house of David will be like God, like the Angel of the LORD going before them. On that day I will set out to destroy all the nations that attack Jerusalem." Zech 12:3-9 NIV (Emphasis Mine)

"Behold, a day is coming for the LORD when the spoil taken from you will be divided among you. For I will gather all the nations against Jerusalem to battle, and the city will be captured, the houses plundered, the women ravished and half of the city exiled, but the rest of the people will not be cut off from the city. Then the LORD will go forth and fight against those nations, as when He fights on a day of battle. In that day His feet will stand on the Mount of Olives, which is in front of Jerusalem on the east; and the Mount of Olives will be split in its middle from east to west by a very large valley, so that half of the mountain will move toward the north and the other half toward the south. You will flee by the valley of My mountains, for the valley of the mountains will reach to Azel; yes, you will flee just as you fled before the earthquake in the days of Uzziah king of Judah. Then the LORD, my God, will come, and all the holy ones with Him!" Zech 14:1-5

When were these passages fulfilled? They weren't. And neither were all the other predictions of the Hebrew Prophets regarding Israel and Jerusalem at the end of the age. How does Preterism deal with them? The answer is simple. They rely on something called Replacement Theology which teaches that Israel was rejected by God and replaced by the Church. This has been used as an excuse to persecute the Jews throughout the centuries. Replacement Theology celebrates all the words of the Prophets concerning the literal destruction of Israel and

Jerusalem, but robs and steals her of all the prophecies of restoration, making them non-literal and applying them now to the Church. This is a blatant disregard for Scripture and an attack on the Jewish people, but it continues to be spoken day after day in books and messages as though it was absolute truth, even among those who say they believe in the state of Israel's redemption. How can this still be going on, especially now, since all that the Prophets have spoken about the restoration of Israel is literally coming to pass? Indeed, a great sifting of hearts has come to the Church on this issue. Listen carefully to the spirit behind Preterism:

"The Book of Revelation is not about the Second Coming of Christ. It is about the destruction of Israel and Christ's victory over His enemies in the establishment of the New Covenant Temple. In fact, as we shall see, the word coming as used in the Book of Revelation never refers to the Second Coming. Revelation prophesies the judgment of God on apostate Israel; and while it does briefly point to events beyond its immediate concerns, that is done merely as a 'wrap-up,' to show that the ungodly will never prevail against Christ's Kingdom. But the main focus of Revelation is upon events which were soon to take place."[140] *(Emphasis Mine)*

When Jesus came down the Mount of Olives on what we call Palm Sunday, He saw the destruction of the city and the nation of Israel and He wept. Surely He understood the long exile that they would go through and how He would be reconciled to them again at the end of the age! Of course He did. And when He poured out His wrath on them from 66-72 AD, was He not weeping? But these people say that despite the words of the Prophets toward His beloved people, Messiah could find no

---

[140] *The Days of Vengeance: An Exposition of the Book of Revelation* by David Chilton

mercy for them in his heart, destroyed them as enemies, and condemned them never to be a nation again, contrary to His solemn promises.[141] Yet Gentiles, on the other hand, whom God has equally promised to pour out his wrath on, are spared. And of course, the apostate Gentile Church is forgiven, and released from all judgment, and is now being restored. Did she not also pollute the earth with evil for nearly 2,000 years? How convenient and how anti-Semitic!

It is very clear in the New Testament, that the 1st Century Church did not share this view, and it is equally clear from history that the 2nd Century Church did not share it either.

"I say then, they did not stumble so as to fall, did they? May it never be! But by their transgression salvation has come to the Gentiles, to make them jealous. Now if their transgression is riches for the world and their failure is riches for the Gentiles, how much more will their fulfillment be!" Romans 11:11-12

"For I do not want you, brethren, to be uninformed of this mystery -- so that you will not be wise in your own estimation -- that a partial hardening has happened to Israel until the fullness of the Gentiles has come in; and so all Israel will be saved; just as it is written, 'THE DELIVERER WILL COME FROM ZION, HE WILL REMOVE UNGODLINESS FROM JACOB. THIS IS MY COVENANT WITH THEM, WHEN I TAKE AWAY THEIR SINS.' From the standpoint of the gospel they are enemies for your sake, but from the standpoint of God's choice they are beloved for the sake of the fathers; for the gifts and the calling of God are irrevocable." Romans 11:25-29

Since when have we been freed from following the teaching and

---

[141] Jer 31:35-37

practice of the Early Church? Isn't that Scripture? If they were Premillennialists (and they were), what right do we have to reject their teaching? Shouldn't that be enough for us?

Replacement Theology is a doctrine of hell. It contradicts not only the content of Scripture, but the heart of it as well -- not to mention it maligns the character and reputation of God Almighty. Therefore, any doctrine built on it is rotten to the core. Furthermore, anyone who teaches or promotes Preterism does not love Israel, no matter how much they say so, or how many tours they've been on.

Though Premillennialists are quick to say they do not believe in Replacement Theology, many of them are still teaching and preaching it. It still affects the way they approach Scripture. This is one reason they are so easily led to Preterism. If you truly embrace God's Word concerning Israel and how it is being fulfilled today, you cannot fall prey to this teaching.

2. Private or Non-Literal Interpretation of Scripture

"But know this first of all, that no prophecy of Scripture is a matter of one's own interpretation, for no prophecy was ever made by an act of human will, but men moved by the Holy Spirit spoke from God. But false prophets also arose among the people, just as there will also be false teachers among you, who will secretly introduce destructive heresies, even denying the Master who bought them, bringing swift destruction upon themselves." 2 Peter 1:20-2:1

The context of this Scripture is clearly End-Time teaching. The whole book is about false teachers who lack character, and, having gone astray from the faith, are saying, "Where is the promise of His coming?" Peter tells us that the coming (Greek *parousia*, "presence, coming") and revealing of Jesus to the world in Glory and Majesty, that was prophesied by the prophets (1:19), is on track, even though some think it is taking too long. He also calls this *parousia*, the Day of Lord.

"But the day of the Lord will come like a thief, in which the heavens will pass away with a roar and the elements will be destroyed with intense heat, and the earth and its works will be burned up." 2 Peter 3:10

The Day of the Lord judgment which is coming upon the world is a primary theme of the Prophets of Israel (Joel 2:31, Isaiah 2, 13:9-13, and many more). Incidentally, it is not the time of destruction upon Israel which took place in the 1st Century. It is a time of judgment on the earth when all the wicked will be destroyed.

"The sun will be dark when it rises and the moon will not shed its light. Thus I will punish the world for its evil and the wicked for their iniquity..." Is 13:10-11NASU

Peter, of course, being a good student of the Prophets, knew this and affirms it in Chapter 2, verse 9:

"....then the Lord knows how to rescue the godly from temptation, and to keep the unrighteous under punishment for the day of judgment..." 2 Peter 2:9

Now, regarding the words of the Prophets and all Scripture for that matter, Peter says that it is not a matter of one's own private interpretation. This means that the words of the Prophets have a literal meaning which cannot be taken away or reinterpreted by us. The literal and plain meaning of the authors of the Bible is not to be overwritten by anyone. This was the practice of the false teachers in the 1ˢᵗ Century, and it is the practice of false teachers today as well. Though it is clear that there is often a prophetic truth to be gleaned from a passage, or a moral application to be made, there is never a license or justification to make a change in the plain, literal meaning of the author. The only time we can interpret a passage non-literally is when the text makes it clear that it is not to be taken literally. This is not difficult to understand. Text must have a literal meaning and the rules of language insist that words have a literal meaning and application. They cannot be altered or translated as something other than what was written and intended by the author. But those who use their own private interpretation can make the Scripture say whatever they want. This was the practice of the Gnostic false teachers in Peter's day, and it is the predominant way in which the Bible is interpreted today by Charismatics, and even more so in the Revival Movement. I know, since I am part of both, and throughout my Christian walk this has grieved me. This, in my opinion, is the primary reason, besides Replacement Theology, that we have so much confusion and heresy.

Those who read the Bible non-literally and are always looking for the allegorical or figurative meaning, reduce it to a series of stories and magic sayings, and reject its authority and orthodoxy. Without this method of "interpretation," Preterism cannot exist. Only Premillennialism relies on a straightforward literal reading of Scripture. Preterism considers the Old Testament literal, and fulfilled in the destruction of Jerusalem. But the rest of the Bible it conveniently interprets non-literally. Who gives them the authority to do this? This position undermines Scripture and the will of God for today.

Conclusion
Every prophecy of Scripture that has come to pass has done so literally. Over 300 specific prophecies about Jesus were walked

out in the most minute detail. His crucifixion is outlined in Psalm 22 and Isaiah 53. The striking of Jesus and the scattering of His disciples is detailed in Zechariah 13. The betrayal of Jesus by Judas for thirty pieces of silver, is foretold in Zechariah 11 and fulfilled to the letter. The prophets, including Jesus, prophesied the destruction of Jerusalem, with the siege and the worldwide scattering of the nation in 70 AD, which came to pass in an extraordinary literal way. How then can anyone suggest the rest of Bible prophecy is not to be fulfilled literally, but somehow already happened in a "spiritual," figurative sense? Please understand, this is not just an eschatological point of view; it is an aberration, a departure from reality, from logic, and from the clear teaching of the Word of God. Jesus prophesied the destruction of Jerusalem in Luke 21, which came to pass literally. But His prophecy did not end there. He said that Jerusalem would be trodden down by Gentile rulers and restored to Israeli rule at the end of the age. This too has been fulfilled literally in 1967. In the same way, the Tribulation period will take place, and will fulfill all the horrendous prophecies spoken about it, in minute detail. Those who ignore this reality will find their dominion rhetoric of little help when the day comes and they are caught in a trap.[142]

For decades, Charismatics and Pentecostals ignored sound eschatology and used silly, ignorant excuses to avoid the subject. They mocked those of us who held down the fort, calling us "escapists" and "doom and gloom idiots." Now their children are paying a heavy price and going into spiritual exile for lack of knowledge.[143] The mocking and scoffing has turned to hate as this new generation of radicals has embraced the wrong cause. Someday soon, the mocking will be replaced with fright and terror when many realize the monster they have

---

[142] Luke 21:34
[143] Isaiah 5:13

created. Dear Friend, make no mistake about it, your eschatology impacts what you do and where you will go. This is not simply a matter of different opinions. One position is Biblical and prepares for the return of Christ. The others are opposed to Scripture, have no longing for His appearing, and those who embrace them do so at their own peril.

Chapter Seven
It's All Panning Out

The teaching of Preterism is so unhinged from Scripture and reality that it is hard to understand how godly people came up with it. It is even harder, however, to understand how Premillennialists can put it in their eschatological sandwich. How did this happen, you may ask? How did they get to the place where they blend two conflicting worldviews? The answer lies in what has become an obsession with the Church and its importance in the world, rather than a preoccupation with Christ and an undistracted devotion to Him alone.[144] The Early Church was admonished to be alert and awake for His return (not the destruction of Jerusalem),[145] but now they say such expectation is self-focused and lacking in vision. Paul told believers to set their minds on things above, not on things of the earth.[146] But they say we must be preoccupied with transforming culture and making earth heaven. He also admonished us to serve the living God and wait for His Son from heaven.[147] But they say we are to stop waiting and take the kingdom now, because Jesus already came or is stranded in heaven waiting for us. What foolishness -- what arrogance! How has this generation of Christian leaders become so attached to the world?

The rise of Preterism is a direct result of the failure of Premillennialists to value the teaching of Scripture more than their personal dreams and ambitions. Rather than wasting their time listening, or being sharpened by the Word and each other, they chose instead to let their agenda drive the narrative. This process began in the eighties, became a vacuum in the nineties,

---

[144] 2Cor 11:2-3
[145] Mt 24:42-44, 25:13,
[146] Col 3:1-3
[147] 1 Thess 1:9-10

and is now being filled with false teaching and heresy that is "making perfect sense" and "answering all their questions." Since I have been around all this time and have watched this progression with my own eyes, I would like to summarize what I consider to be the attitude behind this eschatological nosedive.

Rediscovering the Rapture

In the early days of the Charismatic Movement, virtually everyone was a Premillennialist. I remember the general excitement that was palpable regarding the soon coming of Christ. There was, however, always disagreement about the timing of the Rapture, and by and large, Charismatics were drawn to a Post-Trib view. I espoused this position for 20 years and was unwilling to even consider the Pre-Trib scenario. I generally viewed it as escapist and promoting a disengaged, disinterested Church looking merely to go to heaven, rather than fulfilling the call of God. My mentors at the time were always going on about the Dispensationalists,[148] and how their system was off. There were two things about Dispensationalism that offended me and my peers. First the idea that the Rapture could happen at any moment, and second the lack of concern they seemed to have for what God was doing in restoring the Church. However, I never doubted Premillennialism, and there was always an excitement in my heart regarding the end of the age and the return of Christ. When revival hit me in 1994, my eyes were opened to how Church-centered I had become and how I had lost my first love. It was during this time that Christ Himself became the focus of my attention and affection once again, and when I began to reconsider my attitude concerning the Rapture. I read the Scriptures over and over, for a two-year period, until I had clarity on the issues that troubled me. I never considered any of the other Millennial views, other than

---

[148] Dispensationalism is the idea of different dispensations of God's working with human beings, i.e. the dispensation of Law, the dispensation of grace, etc.

Premillennialism, since I had looked at those before and found them to be not only unbiblical, but nonsensical as well. I did not become a Dispensationalist, though there are good points in that view, but I fail to understand why Charismatic and Revival leaders assume that to believe in a Pre-Trib Rapture, one must be a Dispensationalist. This is really a cop out and an excuse to thrash the concept of the Rapture. Nevertheless, I concluded through my studies that the Rapture cannot come, as Paul stated clearly, until the Apostasy comes first and the Man of Lawlessness (Antichrist) is revealed. This happens in the middle of Daniel's 70th Week, when the Tribulation begins. Thus, I also believe that the Rapture is real and is Pre-Trib. Indeed, that is the whole point of it. For more on this Premillennialist view, see my book, *The 7 Lost Keys of End-Time Prophecy*.[149]

While I was reconsidering my point of view on the Rapture, it seems many of my colleagues were becoming even stronger in their disdain for Dispensationalism. And there are two main reasons for their overreaction: hatred for the Rapture, which they consider "escapist," and a preoccupation with the Church and its glory. These two issues, over time, coupled with embarrassing and often illogical predictions by Dispensationalists, have caused many Premillennialists, especially those in the Apostolic Movement, to become cynical regarding eschatology. Thus, they are wide open to an alternate view that validates them and fits their presupposed agenda. It's as though they have become obsessed with worldly conquest and recognition to somehow prove themselves to the Lord. Let us consider these two issues now, in hopes that we can prevent more Premillennialists from making a tragic mistake.

---

[149] *The 7 Lost Keys of End-Time Prophecy*, by PJ Hanley, available at Amazon.com

Hatred for the Rapture

"Be on guard, that your hearts may not be weighted down with dissipation and drunkenness and the worries of life, and that day come on you suddenly like a trap; for it will come upon all those who dwell on the face of all the earth. But keep on the alert at all times, praying in order that you may have strength to escape all these things that are about to take place, and to stand before the Son of Man." Luke 21:36

Jesus Himself was the first in the New Testament to teach on the concept of escaping. The "day" he is referring to here is not a 24-hour period, but the Day of the Lord, or the Tribulation, at the end of the age. This is clear from the fact that He says it will come upon "all who dwell on the face of the earth," will include the shaking of the heavens, the visible return of Christ in glory, and was spoken to the generation that would see all the End-Time events take place. Premillennialists who believe in the Post-Trib Rapture view have scurried to find another meaning for the Greek word *ekpheugó* that is translated "escape" in all reliable translations.[150] But why? What is so offensive about the idea of escaping? Nothing, especially if Christ is initiating the plan. Indeed, even if you don't believe the Rapture is Pre-Trib, there is still no reason to hate the idea of Christ coming to take His followers to be with Him. It is one thing to not be able to see a Rapture before the Tribulation, but it is quite another thing to hate it. Indeed, the writings of many in the Apostolic Movement, Premillennials included, suggest that if they had proof that the rapture was Pre-Trib, they would still loathe it.

"The doctrine of the rapture was a great and effective ruse of the enemy to implant in the church a retreat mentality, but it will

---

[150] See also Acts 16:27, Rom 2:3, 2 Cor 11:33 for other uses of the word *ekpheugó*

not succeed. Already this yoke has been cast off by the majority in the advancing church, and it will soon be cast off by all..."[151]

What has happened to the Revival Movement that longing for the Bridegroom, and desiring to be with Him where He is, has become offensive to them? And who says that belief in the Pre-Trib Rapture causes complacency or a "retreat mentality?" That is absolute nonsense. Those who are genuinely awaiting the return of Christ and believe it is near, are undoubtedly more motivated than those who think the Church must conquer the world before He comes. After 40 years of ministering to the Church, I find this view depressing and hopeless, not to mention unscriptural.

"Beloved, now we are children of God, and it has not appeared as yet what we will be. We know that when He appears, we will be like Him, because we will see Him just as He is. And everyone who has this hope fixed on Him purifies himself, just as He is pure." 1 John 3:2-3 (Emphasis Mine)

Can you hear the excitement in John's words, and the proof of what he was living for? It seems it was not social transformation. He already told us that the world was judged and passing away. He reminds us of what our hope is to be fixed upon -- the return of Christ. And that no one who has this hope will be nonchalant about living for Him. However, some today consider this hope to be misguided, and think it more fitting for believers to be focused on how we can change the world.

"This study of last things is also important to revival. I believe we are going to see a turning from a doom-and-gloom view of the end-times (the day of the Lord and Jesus' return), in which

---

[151] *The Harvest* 1989 /1990 revised booklet on pg.121

we expect the church to be lukewarm, to an end-times view of hope, purpose, victory and great revival. I believe we will move into a more Biblical view that is based on understanding that the kingdom of God is ever-increasing and ever-expanding. This characteristic of the kingdom is seen in Jesus' parables in Matthew 13: the mustard seed growing and the yeast affecting the entire lump of dough."[152] (Emphasis and Parenthesis Mine)

What has happened to those who, in the early days of the revival, wanted to dance on the streets that are golden? What is so doom and gloom about the return of Jesus and the Day of the Lord? I cannot discern what Randy believes. He seems to be suggesting that there is no Tribulation coming. Indeed, he even sounds like a Preterist or an Amillennialist. Yet on his webpage, under what he believes, I find clear Premillennialist doctrine. What confusion! I pray he discovers that a Bride truly awaiting her Bridegroom is the most motivated to do the Kingdom work.

"I will not allow any interpretation of the Scriptures that destroys hope for the nations and undermines our command to restore ruined cities."[153]

There is no command anywhere to restore ruined cities. In Isaiah 58, God speaks about the remnant of Israel restoring the ruined cities, and even to them it is not a command.[154] "I will not allow." With all the ruined cities in California alone, it looks like Jesus is stranded for some time. Folks, they call this an eschatology of hope! Can you believe it?

"Is it possible that things are getting better in the world? (Only if one is in complete denial.) The Bible says that there will be no

---

[152] *Where is Revival Headed?* Randy Clark, Charisma 1/7/2013

[153] Charisma Magazine, *8-Eschatological-Core-Values*, Kris Vallotton, 11/30/2015

[154] Is 58: 12, 61:4, Amos 9:14, Ezek 36:10

end to the increase of God's government or of peace (Isaiah 9:7). What if things are evolving instead of eroding?"[155] (Parenthesis Mine)

"How has this played out? The human race is enormously better off now than it was when Jesus died and was raised from the dead 2,000 years ago! satan is losing ground more and more rapidly. Those who think the world is getting worse and worse are missing the big picture of human history. I now regard my former Pre-tribulationism and Premillenialism as escapist eschatology. I do not plan to give any territory back to satan or his Antichrist. Yes, there will be setbacks, but the advances will far outnumber them. Instead of an escapist eschatology, I espouse a victorious eschatology![156]

It is hard to imagine how such intelligent, smart, scholarly people, can read the Bible and live in this sin-sick world, and yet conclude that everything is getting better. What are they smoking? What is the problem? Why are these Premillennialists so confused? And why are they so out of step with the Church that was established and launched by Christ Himself?

Blessed be the God and Father of our Lord Jesus Christ, who according to His great mercy has caused us to be born again to a living hope through the resurrection of Jesus Christ from the dead, to obtain an inheritance which is imperishable and undefiled and will not fade away, reserved in heaven for you, who are protected by the power of God through faith for a salvation (deliverance)[157]ready to be revealed in the last time." 1 Pet 1:3-5 (Emphasis and Parenthesis Mine)

_____

[155] Is It the End of The World as We Know It? Kris Vallotton, December 5, 2016
[156] Why You Must Take Dominion Over Everything, C Peter Wagner, Charisma News, 12/5/2012
[157] The Greek word sótéria can also be translated "deliverance" which is more appropriate here.

Peter was not expecting things to get better -- quite the contrary. Neither was he talking about the end of the Old Covenant age as the End-Time. He was telling the Church to focus on what was reserved for them in heaven, and the hope of their deliverance which was to take place at the end of the age, known to us as the Rapture. He was not talking about being saved from their sins and being made right with God, since they already had that salvation, but a deliverance that was to come in the "last time." In the Greek, it is *kairo eschatou* (the Greek word from which we get "Eschatology"), meaning the specific End-Time. To suggest that he was talking about 70 AD is balmy, since there was no deliverance in 70 AD for the believers scattered throughout Pontus, Galatia, Cappadocia, Asia, and Bithynia, to whom the letter is written. Furthermore, those who doubt that this deliverance is the Rapture must explain what other deliverance for believers is spoken of as occurring at end of the age. Regardless of your view concerning the Rapture, the believers were being told to look up toward heaven for their hope of the future, and not to some great revival that was to come on earth. Also, lest you miss the point, it is emphasized again in verse 13, where Peter tells believers that they should fix their hope completely on this salvation that is to come, when Christ is revealed.

"Therefore, prepare your minds for action, keep sober in spirit, fix your hope completely on the grace to be brought to you at the revelation of Jesus Christ." 1Pet 1:13 (Emphasis Mine)

There is no doubt that many who believe in the Rapture have an "escapist mentality," which I understand to mean they are unconcerned about the work of Christ on the earth. However, to suggest that is the case because they believe in the Rapture is nonsense. It is just an excuse for their complacency. Indeed, there are many complacent Christians who don't believe in the

Rapture, including a large chunk of the so-called "apostolic churches" that are complacent. Surely no one can suggest that Peter, or the believers he was addressing, were complacent, or became complacent, because of the Apostle's exhortation? And what about Paul? Was he complacent? He too had his hope in the deliverance to come, and not some worldwide awakening to the gospel, something he himself was at the forefront of when he wrote these verses.

"For (because) our citizenship is in heaven, from which also we eagerly wait for a Savior (deliverer), the Lord Jesus Christ; who will transform the body of our humble state into conformity with the body of His glory, by the exertion of the power that He has even to subject all things to Himself." Phil 3:20-21 (Emphasis and Parenthesis Mine)

Paul says that our citizenship is in heaven (which de-emphasizes a fulfillment here on earth), and that we "eagerly wait" for *a* savior or deliverer (not *the* Savior), who is the Lord Jesus Christ, who will transform our bodies into His image. Who can deny this is the Rapture? Nevertheless, it is abundantly clear that Paul, who preached the gospel throughout the Roman Empire and did many extraordinary miracles, was not looking to some worldwide takeover of the Church before the return of Christ. On the contrary, his hope was firmly fixed on the Rapture, the upward call to be with Christ, and he was determined to be in that number whether dead or alive.[158]

Jesus said the following regarding the signs of the end of the age:

---

[158] Phil 3:11-14

"But when these things begin to take place, straighten up and lift up your heads, because your redemption is drawing near." Luke 21:28

Follow these instructions right now, go ahead, and see where your eyes will be. Jesus wanted the Church of the Last Days looking up and not down.

The author of Hebrews said this:

"...Christ also, having been offered once to bear the sins of many, shall appear a second time for salvation (deliverance) without reference to sin, to those who eagerly await Him." Heb 9:28 (Emphasis and Parenthesis Mine)

Once again, the true apostolic message is to be eagerly waiting or awaiting the return and deliverance of Christ, a return that has nothing to do with sin, which rules out 70 AD and Revelation 19. This is the gathering in the air, at the beginning of the Tribulation. Is this the attitude or message of these new apostles? Hardly! Their teaching and posture is not only contrary, if it were applied to the Church of the New Testament, they would be indicted as a bunch of heavenly-minded escapists.

"Let us hold fast the confession of our hope without wavering, for He who promised is faithful; and let us consider how to stimulate one another to love and good deeds, not forsaking our own assembling together, as is the habit of some, but encouraging one another; and all the more, as you see the day drawing near." Heb 10:23-25 (Emphasis Mine)

The hope that is mentioned here, which we are to hold onto and confess, is outlined in the previously quoted verse from

Hebrews 9:28. This is the Rapture which is to take place at the beginning of the Day of the Lord.[159] This is the day that we are to look for and see approaching, and encourage one another with in our frequent meetings and, should I say, conferences. When was the last time you went to a conference like that?

Obsession with the Church

From its inception, the Charismatic Movement brought with it a focus on the restoration of the Church. We understood that revival didn't just come to make the Church more alive in Christ, but there was also a restoration of Biblical truth that had been lost. Indeed, one can say that since the reformation, the Church has been in a continual state of revival and restoration of truth, which accelerated greatly in the last century. During the eighties and early nineties, we understood this series of revival waves to be restoring to us both the theology and practice of the New Testament Church. Consequently, we understood that the power present in the Early Church would also be restored to the Church at the end of the age. However, somewhere along the line, and largely due to confused eschatology, the concept of revival and awakening of the Church evolved into a promise of mass conversion of cities and nations. Stories about past revivals were told, where people all around were coming under conviction and falling on their knees repenting. What is generally left out, of course, is that these towns and villages were largely filled with God-fearing people who were believers in Christ, though backslidden in many ways. The situation today in the Western nations is very different. Nevertheless, the notion of a large-scale Christian awakening of the whole world has become the mantra, and rallying cry for the Church, especially Charismatics. This so-called promise of awakening and harvest, coupled with the view of a victorious End-Time Church (with

---

159 2 Thess 2:1-4

which I agree), is the bait that makes Premillennialists swallow Dominionism and even Preterism. However, no such promise exists in Scripture. There is a great harvest that comes to the Lord during the Tribulation period, but the impetus seems more to do with trial than some apostolic reformation.[160] Let's take a moment, then, to examine some of these dramatic and often wild predictions about the discipling of nations coming from the Apostolic Movement.

"My favorite term is 'dominion eschatology.' Why? Because Jesus did not give His Great Commission in vain. The battle will be ferocious, and we will suffer some casualties along the way. However, we will continue to push satan back and disciple whole nations. We are aggressively retaking dominion, and the rate at which this is happening will soon become exponential. The day will come when 'The kingdoms of this world have become the kingdoms of our Lord and of His Christ, and He shall reign forever and ever.' (Rev. 11:15) NKJV"[161]

Mr. Wagner was a Partial Preterist and a Dominionist. He reinterpreted Jesus' commission to be about the discipling of national entities, instead of the obvious meaning, which is to make disciples of the Gentile peoples. This reinterpretation implies a takeover and ruling of nations ("aggressively retaking dominion"), which was not advocated by Christ or any of His Apostles. The proof is in the way Jesus' Apostles, and even Jesus Himself, operated and lived their lives. All of them submitted to earthly authorities even to the point of death, and never tried to take over any governments, but devoted themselves to preaching the gospel and teaching the new converts as they were instructed to do. Furthermore, Partial

---

[160] Rev 7:14-17
[161] *Why You Must Take Dominion Over Everything*, C Peter Wagner, Charisma News, 12/5/2012

Preterists believe that almost the entire book of Revelation was fulfilled in 70 AD or thereabouts. If that is true, the kingdoms of this world became the Kingdom of our Lord and Christ at that time. Thus, there should not be any need for the Church to make it happen now!

"All fivefold ministers must function until Christ's Church is a fully restored Church, a glorious spotless Church, an overcoming-all-things Church, which subdues all Christ's enemies and places them under His feet. If the rapture of the Church takes place before this is accomplished, then declaration would have to be made that these Scriptures failed to come to pass, or the apostles, prophets and other fivefold ministries have to continue their ministry after the rapture until these Scriptures are fulfilled." [162]

Dr. Hamon seems to have blended Premillennialism and Postmillennialism into a concoction with a heavy Latter Rain[163] flavor. It is true that all genuine believers are sons of God, and that we are to walk as Jesus walked, yet Dr. Hamon seems to have taken that to an extreme. He seems to literally believe that the Church is going to be bodily transformed, and move in such power that they will subdue the nations and all of Christ's enemies.

"At that time the sons of God will be fully manifested on the earth. Widespread spiritual warfare will result with the Sons of God doing battle with satan and company, the non-Christian nations of this world will also be defeated. Once the earth has been subdued, Jesus will come back to earth and be given the

---

[162] Dr. Bill Hamon, *Apostles and Prophets and the Coming Moves of God;* (Destiny Image: Shippensburg PA, 1997) p 146.

[163] The Latter Rain revival began in Saskatchewan, Canada, in 1948. I believe it was a genuine revival, but because of pride and a heavy Replacement Theology understanding of Scripture, it quickly got derailed.

Kingdom that has been won for Him by this "manchild company."[164]

"When the Church realizes its full sonship, its bodily redemption will cause a redemptive chain reaction throughout all of creation."[165]

"The Body of Christ will become too powerful in the supernatural power of God for the ungodly to be able to restrict or to destroy them."[166]

"The Church will gain victory over the last enemy, death. Victory speaks of a battle being fought. The last day saints will wage and win a warfare against death. The last generation saints will come to translating faith in preparation for participation in the translation."[167]

Dr. Hamon is preaching a full takeover by the Church before Jesus comes, including the conquering of death. Therefore, it is unclear how he can still be a Premillennialist. He seems to be saying that the sons of God are fully manifested with immortal glorious bodies, and so powerful that no one can contend with them. It is not clear if he means this will happen to the whole Church or just the elite apostles. In any event, it's bizarre. Isn't it time somebody sat with this dear man and set him straight? Where are the apostles when you need them?

"The Lord is coming back for a glorious church, he's coming back for an overcoming church, a church that is the head and not the tail, above and not beneath, a church that knows how to

---

[164] *Prophets and the Prophetic Movement,* by Bill Hamon
[165] Bill Hamon, *The Eternal Church,* p.385
[166] Ibid, p.363
[167] Bill Hamon, *The Eternal Church,* P.349

possess and occupy. Our good friend Lance Wallnau is going to share a message with you today on the seven mountains that are available for the church to conquer, and conquer we will!"[168]

"Those in this camp (he means dispensationalists) believe they have to passively wait for the rapture and avoid political and social reform, because trying to transform culture is like 're-arranging the chairs on the Titanic.' This is based on a faulty reading of Scriptures such as Daniel 9:24-27. Although I do not believe every nation and all people will be saved before the second bodily return of Christ, I do believe there will be some sort of strong kingdom influence in the nations (especially 'sheep nations;' read Matt. 25:32) before the second coming. All of the major Biblical covenants and themes point to a victorious Church and victorious gospel before the end of human history (read Gen. 1:28; 12:1-3; 22:17-18; Ps. 110:2; Acts 3:21)."[169] *(Parenthesis Mine)*

First of all, to suggest that those who are eagerly waiting for the return of Christ and the Rapture are passive toward God's work is outrageous. As we have seen, Peter and Paul encouraged us to be "eagerly awaiting" the Rapture, and they certainly weren't passive. I look forward to the Rapture. It is my blessed hope, but I am definitely not passive. When Paul confronted the Thessalonians about their fear that they had missed the Day of the Lord and the Rapture, he did not tell them to forget about the Rapture and focus on taking dominion. Not at all. He simply set them straight on timing. Secondly, in the above quote from Mr. Mattera, he admits that he is a Premillennialist but then misleads people with a subtle twist on the parable of the sheep and the goats found in Matthew 25. Jesus said that when He returns and sets up His Throne in Jerusalem He will gather the

---

[168] Patricia King introducing Lance Wallnau, http://vimeo.com/1786357
[169] *12 Teachings That Harm the Church,* by Joseph Mattera, Charisma, 7/14/2015,

survivors from the nations before Him to be judged. He is not going to separate them as national entities with their banners and so forth. That's ridiculous! A straightforward reading of the text would not support that -- it must be superimposed on it. But the NAR has reinvented the meaning of "all the nations" in this passage, as they also have in Matthew 28:19. They are dead wrong, of course, as is clearly illustrated when we see what happens. Jesus does not say, "America on my right," "Iran on my left," or anything like that. That kind of thinking suggests that every person in America would be considered a sheep, and everyone in Iran would be a goat. That is completely impossible. What Jesus is clearly saying is that He will gather together the survivors of the various nations, and separate them as individuals – sheep from goats, based on how they have treated His brothers (the Jews & possibly Christians) during the Tribulation.

This idea of whole nations repenting and coming to Christ is not promised anywhere in Scripture. In fact, it's the opposite – a remnant will be saved. These folks make it sound like there are whole nations around the world that are given to Christ, and standing with Him, from the government down, during the Tribulation period, under the domain of Antichrist. This is not the picture presented in the Bible. It is a time of great trial for the whole earth, and the multitudes who come to Christ do so under great stress and loss of life. Indeed, the vast majority of believers are martyred. Consider the words of Jesus regarding what the earth is like when He comes:

"…now, will not God bring about justice for His elect who cry to Him day and night, and will He delay long over them? "I tell you that He will bring about justice for them quickly. However, when the Son of Man comes, will He find faith on the earth?" Luke 18:7-8 (Emphasis Mine)

Why would Jesus ask this question if He were expecting a "strong Kingdom influence" among the nations?

"Enter through the narrow gate; for the gate is wide and the way is broad that leads to destruction, and there are many who enter through it. For the gate is small and the way is narrow that leads to life, and there are few who find it." Mt 7:13-14

Has that reality of few finding life changed? Did I miss an announcement somewhere?

"Behold, a day is coming for the Lord when the spoil taken from you will be divided among you. For I will gather all the nations against Jerusalem to battle, and the city will be captured, the houses plundered, the women ravished and half of the city exiled, but the rest of the people will not be cut off from the city. Then the Lord will go forth and fight against those nations, as when He fights on a day of battle." Zech 14:1-3 (Emphasis Mine)

To the Preterist, I say, when did this battle take place? And to the Premillennial Dominionist, I say, if there are all these Christian nations at the end of the age, why is the Lord gathering their armies to Jerusalem for judgment?

"For the coming of the Son of Man will be just like the days of Noah. For as in those days which were before the flood they were eating and drinking, they were marrying and giving in marriage, until the day that Noah entered the ark, and they did not understand until the flood came and took them all away; so shall the coming of the Son of Man be." Mt 24:37-39 (Emphasis Mine)

"Like the days of Noah" does not sound like a great awakening has occurred! It's a time of judgment when the righteous are delivered and judgment falls on the wicked.

"Therefore just as the tares are gathered up and burned with fire, so shall it be at the end of the age. The Son of Man will send forth His angels, and they will gather out of His kingdom all stumbling blocks, and those who commit lawlessness, and will cast them into the furnace of fire; in that place there shall be weeping and gnashing of teeth. Then THE RIGHTEOUS WILL SHINE FORTH AS THE SUN in the kingdom of their Father. He who has ears, let him hear." Mt 13:40-43 (Emphasis Mine)

Please notice the word "then." It means "at that time," when the wicked have been judged that the righteous will shine forth as the sun in the Kingdom – the Millennial Reign.

"Another part of the problem is doctrine. Many people have felt that the world should get progressively worse before Jesus returns to save it. I am aware that the subject of reforming nations brings up the question of my end-time eschatological stance. Truthfully, my heart is so focused on "doing business and occupying" (see Luke 19:13) until He comes that I haven't fully grappled with this issue. I want to see millions from across the Middle East, Africa, Asia, and other lands worshiping before the throne of God because of sweeping revivals. I also believe that it is my mandate as a believer to see that the nations are discipled and taught of the Lord. My preacher daddy had this stance on the end times: "Honey," he said with a smile, "I'm not a post-millennialist or a pre-millennialist -- I'm a pan-millennialist! I believe it will all 'pan out' in the end!" I'm following in his footsteps on this. Others much brighter than I *am and dedicated to the study of eschatology can figure that out.*[170]

Dear Cindy, I believe your desire is sincere, but isn't it time you realized that it is panning out, and you are no longer teaching Premillennialism. Your daddy was living at a different time, and your spiritual daddy left the End-Time camp altogether. Sadly, Cindy is typical of Charismatic leaders and pastors who celebrate ignorance of Bible prophecy while at the same time promoting an agenda that is contrary. Her friend and confused Premillennial colleague Lance Wallnau considers the teaching of eschatology to be mischief.

"There is no prevailing apostolic vision to a great degree because of the mischief of eschatology."[171]

Perhaps Lance is getting reacquainted with this mischievous message since he was recently sideswiped by Jonathon Welton. Yet at least Welton knows what he believes, and correctly asserts that Premillennialism (or "Futurism," as they call it) and 7 Mountain conquering are conflicting messages.

"Dr. Lance Wallnau has been publishing a lot of futurism-based eschatology on his newsfeeds. As the major proponent of the Seven Mountains message, this is incongruent with the message God has given him. It will be interesting to see how this develops. It is not sensible to teach that we are to advance the kingdom and take the seven mountains, to then give them back to the antichrist. Dr. Wallnau is brilliant and we wish him the best

---

[170] *The Reformation Manifesto*, Dr. Cindy Jacobs, *Your Part in God's Plan to Change Nations Today*, Baker Publishing

[171] Lance Wallnau, http://www.youtube.com/watch?v=tjq2BuFxM8k&feature=related

and hope that a shift takes place before he loses the ear of his Millennial Generation followers."[172]

I can imagine that by now you are wondering what kind of Church I see at the end of the age. Is it a powerless old hag or a victorious Church? Well, let me make it plain. I believe in the restoration of the Church, and that we should preach the same message, and walk in the same power the Early Church walked in. I have experienced God's power in my life, and continue to experience it daily. I also believe that there is more revival and awakening coming for the true Bride of Christ, who will be victorious over all her enemies, including false teaching. I do not see a conquered Church at the end of the age, but a glorious Church that will be taken to the Bridegroom's side. This Church is an overcoming Church,[173] that is willing to suffer with Him so that she will reign with Him.[174] And since I believe the book of Revelation is future and not already fulfilled, I see this Bridal company as playing a role in the casting down of the devil and his angels from the heavenlies, where she will go to meet her Lord. She overcomes by the Blood of the Lamb, the word of her testimony (the Word of God), and she does not love her life even unto death.[175]

Another thing I want to make clear is that I am not against Christians in politics, nor do I believe that it doesn't matter. As the Church walks with God, we are salt and light, and will have an influence on ungodliness in the world. There is a place for that, but the realm of politics is not to be the focus of the

---

[172] Jonathon Welton, *Apostolic Council on Eschatology, Quarterly*

http://www.endtimecouncil.com/quarterly/global-kingdom-intelligence-forecast-september-2014

[173] Rev 2:7,11,17,26, Rev 3:5,12,21

[174] Rom 8:17, Rev 12:10-12

[175] The 7 Lost Keys of End-Time Prophecy, by PJ Hanley, available at Amazon.com

Church, since we do not have here a lasting city.[176] Many Premillennialists will say they are simply obeying Christ's command to "occupy" until He comes. Of course, they use the King James translation of the Greek word *pragmateuomai*, because it has a military connotation. It suggests conquering and occupying the earthly systems. But that is not the meaning at all. The word *pragmateuomai* means "to trade" and it is translated as "do business" in modern translations. We must remember that Jesus' parable in Luke chapter 19 was illustrating how we must be busy with His work, bearing fruit, as we await His return.

Obsession with Miracles

The NAR apostles have intoxicated themselves with a pursuit of miracles. It's as though they are so desperate to prove themselves and their teaching, that they will stop at nothing to make them happen. Now, let's be clear, miracles are real and are for today. Healings and works of power should be common among us, and we must walk in faith to see them accomplished. However, we are not to pursue miracles, but the Lord Himself, and His presence among us. This pursuit is fleshly and very dangerous. As we are filled with the Holy Spirit and praying for people, we are seeing God do many things. Yet, I think we can all acknowledge that there is more coming. No one is manifesting these miracles at a New Testament level, despite all the hype and hoopla. What is important is that we stay full of the Spirit and walk in the will or agenda of the Father. However, some in their pursuit of their agenda to "bring heaven down," are going astray and dabbling in the Occult. They are

---

[176] Heb 13:14

"reclaiming" New Age practices,[177] and teaching people how to levitate and fly around the room.[178]

Another example of this obsession with miracles was the fiasco that took place at Lakeland, Florida in 2008.[179] Over 400,000 people came from around the world because of the report of miracles. I was pressured myself to go, but felt something wasn't right, so I declined. I have no doubt that God was doing miracles there, and have heard great testimonies, but it was obvious, just from the TV coverage itself, that something was wrong. Later, in the summer, the truth came out regarding Todd Bentley's infidelity and shenanigans, which apparently included drunkenness on stage, and the revival quickly ended. What a shame, and what a blight it has been ever since on the Body of Christ. However, what came out later was the most disturbing. Leaders who had known of previous infidelity had apparently brushed it aside, assuming Mr. Bentley was being pastored, which he clearly wasn't. When the pastor of the church in Lakeland called in the NAR apostles, instead of taking Todd in the back room to find out what was going on, they "formally aligned" him on stage before the whole world. Great words of prophecy were spoken over him about the exploits he would do now that he was aligned. However, a few weeks later it was all uncovered, and the apostles scattered. Later, the presiding apostle claimed that it was the aligning that did the trick and exposed the problems Bentley was having. A year later, Bentley was remarried to one of the young interns who comforted him throughout the revival, because of his marriage break up. It seems that he and his new wife have repented for what they did, and are trying to move on, and that's commendable. However,

[177] See "The Physics of Heaven" by Judy Franklin and Ellyn Davis of Bethel, September 15, 2015
[178] http://www.thenewmystics.com/Groups/1000036249/Home_Page_of/Upcoming_Events/Mystical_Schools/Mystical_Schools.aspx
[179] A miracle revival that occurred with Todd Bentley in Lakeland, Florida, in the Spring of 2008, but which ended in disgrace, because of Bentley's immorality.

did the apostles learn the lesson? There is no evidence they did. This man was in trouble and should not have been on the platform. But the miracles were more important than he and his family were.

Another factor that causes an unhealthy focus on miracles is the teaching that if one is really an apostle, there will be miracles to prove it. This is taken from Paul's words to the Corinthians.

"I have become foolish; you yourselves compelled me. Actually I should have been commended by you, for in no respect was I inferior to the most eminent apostles, even though I am a nobody. The signs of a true apostle were performed among you with all perseverance, by signs and wonders and miracles. For in what respect were you treated as inferior to the rest of the churches, except that I myself did not become a burden to you? Forgive me this wrong!" 2 Cor 12:11-13 (Emphasis Mine)

The above passage is taken from a portion of Scripture where Paul is defending himself and his ministry against charges from others claiming to be apostles, who were slandering him and suggesting that he was not a true apostle of Christ. Indeed, the whole context of this chapter and the previous one is about Paul's defense, and his willingness to even boast about how God was using him, even though he considers this boasting to be foolishness. Yet, he says, even if he does boast, he will be telling the truth and not lying. He reminds the Corinthians that God did great works of power among them, through him. These signs, he says, were proof that he was the real thing, and sent by God. He admits he is acting foolishly by boasting, and this is not advised behavior. Also, it is not known if the other boasters or false apostles[180] had performed any signs, or if Paul was

---

[180] 2 Cor 11:13

comparing his signs to theirs. Nevertheless, it is doubtful that Paul was saying that if one does not have miracles, He has not been sent by God, which of course is the meaning of the word apostle. If that were true, then what do we do with John the Baptist, who, according to Jesus, was a great prophet, yet did no miracles? Besides, I know of no one today, regardless of their claims, who is doing the kind of extraordinary miracles Paul or Peter did, when even his shadow was healing people.[181] Does this mean their ministry is invalid and that they are not apostles? In other words, how far do we go with this? And what about those who are doing miracles, but are not following God's agenda?

"Not everyone who says to Me, 'Lord, Lord,' will enter the kingdom of heaven, but he who does the will of My Father who is in heaven will enter. Many will say to Me on that day, 'Lord, Lord, did we not prophesy in Your name, and in Your name cast out demons, and in Your name perform many miracles?' And then I will declare to them, 'I never knew you; DEPART FROM ME, YOU WHO PRACTICE LAWLESSNESS.'" Mt 7:21-23

This is the most amazing passage. For many years, I must confess, I did not understand it, and wondered why it was even there. It is, in fact, the conclusion of the Sermon on the Mount, which stresses that we must obey the Lord's Word and will to be received by Him. The issue, according to Jesus, is not what we know, or how many miracles we do, but whether or not we are doing the will of the Father. The will of the Father could also be rendered as the agenda of the Father. Thus, what matters is the agenda of the Father. The Lord goes on to say that *many* Christians will come to Him on that day, and rattle on about all the prophecies in His name, and all the demons cast out in His

---

[181] Acts 5:15

163

name, and all the miracles (*many* miracles) they performed in His name, as proof of who they are. These are large and popular ministries. And He will declare that He never knew them, and that they were practicing lawlessness. How astonishing! Why will they be unknown to Christ? Sadly, because they were doing things in His name, real Kingdom stuff, but they were following their own agenda and not His. Besides doing the will of the Father in our own lives, we must be clear on what is the Father's agenda at the end of the age. Thus, our eschatology is paramount if we are to be in the Father's will in these Last Days. It is not enough to have big ministries, to be apostolically aligned, and to be known for miracles if we are in fact opposing the Lord Himself, and preaching or acting contrary to His will!

Conclusion

We began this book with the passage from Ephesians 4 that is commonly used by the NAR to validate its authority and radical claims of a New Apostolic Age. However, there is more in the passage that is almost never quoted, which is to be the result of all this ministry.

"...for the equipping of the saints for the work of service, to the building up of the body of Christ; until we all attain to the unity of the faith, and of the knowledge of the Son of God, to a mature man, to the measure of the stature which belongs to the fullness of Christ. As a result, we are no longer to be children, tossed here and there by waves and carried about by every wind of doctrine, by the trickery of men, by craftiness in deceitful scheming; but speaking the truth in love, we are to grow up in all aspects into Him who is the head, even Christ..." Eph 4:14-15 (Emphasis Mine)

According to Paul, if this great movement of apostles and prophets is genuine, we should be seeing maturity among

God's people, more clarity in the Scriptures, and more unity in the faith. But is this what's happening? No! Christians are more confused than ever, and are bouncing around like hurricane waves in the ocean. False teachings are more plentiful than ever before in history, being spewed out daily, like gadgets from an assembly line. TV preachers and "apostolic" internet sites keep the "faithful" riding the waves of "new revelations," and "supernatural" expectations, while the money piles up in their bank accounts. And no one dares to challenge them for fear of becoming marginalized and banished to the gulag of nonalignment. After all, the Lord wants unity, right? Who would dare be against that? But is this the unity He is looking for? A mishmash, hodge-podge of Biblical truth, doctrines of demons, and supernatural experiences, stirred up together like a bowl of soup, and served with your favorite apostolic ice cream? Certainly not! Real apostles and prophets bring people out of deception and into the unity of *the* faith that was once and for all delivered to the saints.[182]

What, then, is the outcome of all this binding and loosing, prophetic decreeing, apostolic aligning, and 7 Mountain climbing, besides the strangulation and hijacking of the Christian Church? In his book, *Apostles Today* in 2006, the father of the movement admitted the following:

"With this in mind, let's take a look at the state of affairs with regard to our efforts across America toward city transformation. The widespread interest in city transformation began in 1990 with the publication of John Dawson's bestseller, "Taking Our Cities for God." During the decade of the 1990's, virtually every major city in America, launched a city transformation project of one kind or another. Some of the finest of the nation's Christian

---

[182] Jude 3

leadership was involved up-front. A quality library emerged with authors such as, Francis Frangipane, Ed Silvoso, George Otis Jr., Jack Dennison, Jack Hayford, Frank Damazio, and many others joining in to help point the way. Mission America, under the leadership of Paul Cedar, launched a major nationwide project aimed at city transformation. It looked to many of us as if the 1990's would see tangible answers to the prayer, "Thy kingdom come" in city after city. But it didn't happen. In fact, after now more than 15 years of intense effort, it would be difficult to pinpoint a city or even a smaller community in America that has been transformed as a result of proactive, strategic planning. One result of this is that we seem to be experiencing some disturbing sort of transformation fatigue, with some leaders beginning to throw their hands up in despair."[183]

What a sad commentary. Just think of what could have been accomplished, had all this effort and money been put into preaching the gospel to the lost! What if this movement was given to the real Great Commission of winning souls to Christ? What if they had funneled their time and energy into helping local churches do the work of evangelism, rather than spiritual mapping? But instead, countless thousands of believers were taught to spin their wheels in circles, until they got "transformation fatigue." This fatigue apparently influenced Peter Wagner to abandon Premillennial theology for Preterism the same year. What became of the despairing ones, we do not know. But what we do know is that 11 years later, with aligned apostles everywhere, and a gazillion more books on taking cities and transforming nations, there is still nothing to report. There are no transformed cities, towns, villages, or even enclaves. And instead of going back to what works, like evangelizing our friends and neighbors and building up local churches, they are

---

[183] *Apostles Today,* by C. Peter Wagner, Published by Chosen Books, 2006

abandoning the local church for another "new paradigm." Is this not another fad, another transformation project, another wheel-spinning hoax? Is this really the will of God for the Bride of Christ? Is this the agenda of the Father for the Last Days Church? Or is it another agenda, one that is centered in human striving and selfish ambition? Is this movement a reformation of the Church bringing it to maturity, or a counter-reformation leading it to derailment and weeping and gnashing of teeth?

In this book, so far, I have presented abundant evidence concerning the attitude, structure, agenda, and theology of the NAR. It is now up to you to come to your conclusion. In the next chapter, I will tell you why I believe this earthly-focused, politically-minded, social-transformation-obsessed Church may be about to make the ultimate alignment!

"For many walk, of whom I often told you, and now tell you even weeping, that they are enemies of the cross of Christ, whose end is destruction, whose god is their appetite (Lit., belly), and whose glory is in their shame, who set their minds on earthly things." Phil 3:18 (Emphasis and Parenthesis Mine)

Chapter Eight
The Ultimate Alignment

The idea that everything is getting better in the world shocks the minds of reasonable people, and especially believers. It's the kind of thing that comes with massive indoctrination and propaganda, and requires the support and activity of a demonic principality. Having traveled a bit, I can assure you that America is the most "Christian-friendly" country in the world. Yet, in the last two years our nation has embraced gay marriage, something that has never been accepted before in the history of humanity. Our children are being told to change their gender if they don't like the way they were born. A legal war rages in the courts over whether a man who dislikes his gender or is confused can visit the ladies' bathroom or shower stall. We have lost the right to pray in public and the Western world has, for the most part, become anti-Christian and speaks of a Post-Christian era. Islam is rising in every Western nation, and if the Lord tarries, they will rule the world in 50 years. The moral decline and decadence in our country alone, is phenomenal, not to mention everywhere else. War rages in the Middle-East, Christians are slaughtered by ISIS, women are brutalized, and terrorism is increasing. To be sure, God's mercy is still saving people, and the gospel continues to be preached. But to suggest that the world is getting better is insane.[184] Yet a whole new crop of "teachers" from the Revival Movement, who have embraced Preterism, are telling us just that. And what do they point to as proof? The arguments of humanists who reject morality and Christianity.

---

[184] Since this writing we have had the COVID 19 worldwide shutdowns and the rise of an antichrist control system.

"When people see a new story about a natural disaster, or a corrupt politician, you will see Christians hang their heads and say, 'It's just the signs of the times,' implying that the world is on a downward trajectory, and evil should be anticipated. But this assessment of the world is factually wrong. When most major metrics are analyzed, it isn't even open for debate – the world is getting better, not worse."[185]

After making this statement, Mr. Edwards goes on to talk about a decrease in world hunger, and an increase in infant mortality rates, life expectancy, wealth, and literacy. But even if those things were all improving, as he claims, it does not indicate the world is becoming more Christian, or that the Kingdom of God is taking over. What it does suggest is that Christians who view the world this way are falling for the secular humanist lie. They have more in common with the UN, than the Bible-believing Church. Consequently, it is easy to predict which side they will be on as the End-Times (that they don't believe in), unfold.

Apostolic Conundrum

For some time, Charismatic Premillennialists have been mixing Dominionism into their End-Time scenario. Facing the doom and gloom of the Tribulation which strikes fear in people's hearts (without a Rapture promise), they mix it up with a Church in dominion. In other words, they minimize the Tribulation (which cannot be done)[186] and maximize the role of the Church. The two witnesses of Revelation 11 figuratively become an Elijah company representing the Church, which calls down fire on the Antichrist and controls whole towns and cities of believers. One leader told me he sees it sort of like Narnia, with pockets of

---

[185] *7 Reasons Why the World is Getting Better (And Not Worse)*, by Sean Edwards, July 11 2013, on PhilDrysdale.com
[186] Jesus said that had the Tribulation not been cut to 3 ½ years, no life would have been left. He also said nothing like it has happened before or ever will again.

resistance all over the place. Many other Premillennialists have embraced some sort of total dominion, where the Church conquers completely before Jesus comes. However, this is an agenda-driven eschatology that is incompatible with Futurism, not to mention the Bible itself. It's a hybrid mix designed to facilitate a victorious overcoming Church, even though no such Church is pictured in Revelation during the Tribulation – only one that is persecuted and beheaded.[187]

I am not suggesting that one should view the Rapture as I do to be properly prepared for what's coming,[188] but one's posture is key to one's alignment in the Last Days. As we have seen, how we view eschatology is how we will behave during this period. Therefore, the Preterists, with no Tribulation or judgment in the future, and the Premillennial Dominionists who see only a conquering Church, are in grave danger of joining the wrong team. Their apostolic alignment, together with their ambitious agenda, will cause them to form an alliance with the enemies of Christ. Thus, Premillennialists, or Futurists, who persist in their belief that the NAR is a "new wineskin" from God, are facing a serious conundrum in the days ahead.

World Peace

"For you yourselves know full well that the day of the Lord will come just like a thief in the night. While they are saying, 'Peace and safety!' then destruction will come upon them suddenly like labor pains upon a woman with child, and they will not escape."
1 Thess 5:2-3

---

[187]Rev 7:9-17, 12:17, 15:2. There is a victorious remnant pictured in the book of Revelation that is Raptured (Greek, *harpazo*) and taken to be with Christ. See Rev 12:1-17, 14:1-5. Notice the remnant in Rev 14 are not the same as that in Rev 7, as they are taken from among men and are first fruits. Rev 7 is Jews only.

[188] For answers to your questions on the Rapture see, *The 7 Lost Keys of End-Time Prophecy*, by PJ Hanley, available at Amazon.com

The Scriptures are clear that the world will enter a time of peace prior to the Tribulation. But it will only last 3 ½ years. Then all hell will literally break loose. The man of lawlessness, the Antichrist, will be revealed, the earth will be torn asunder, and billions of people will die. When that happens, only the wicked will still be in denial. However, a time of great apostasy precedes the Tribulation. Israel will make a grave error when it makes a peace deal with a world leader who is later revealed as the Antichrist. This will be a peace agreement that will fulfill the Scripture in Daniel 9:27, and usher in the last 7 years of the age. It will regulate Israel's relationship with its neighbors as well as permit the restoration or resumption of Jewish worship on the Temple Mount in Jerusalem. Thus, Israel will embrace this leader as the Messiah.

Though the primary apostasy mentioned by Paul refers to Israel's apostasy,[189] there is also a great apostasy of the Church at the end of the age. This apostasy, or falling away, has already begun, but it will culminate with the backslidden Church leading a world religious body, and rising to power alongside the Antichrist. The framework for this is already in place, and the NAR is paving the way for Charismatic, Pentecostal and Revival churches to participate. They will align together for the agenda of saving the world and "bringing in the Kingdom" which will be perceived as beginning with world peace. Yet, only 3 ½ years into their experiment, the Antichrist will manifest and their treachery will be exposed. Then true believers will come to their senses and realize how they have been deceived, and that destruction has come upon them. This will lead to a great harvest of souls that will come to Christ out of the Tribulation period. Yet, they will suffer greatly.

---

[189] 2 Thess 2:3

This alliance of the Church with the forces of Antichrist in the Last Days was harder to see two decades ago. But now, with the restoration of the social gospel, or gospel of social reformation, it has come clearly into focus. This blending of humanistic concerns with the message of the Kingdom harmonizes perfectly with the agenda of the so-called "mainline churches," who concocted the perfect storm of religion and humanism decades ago. This, coupled with a new determination for unity that downplays theology and orthodoxy, makes the humanistic Kool-Aid tastier. NAR apostles, with their concept of infiltration of systems and governments, and focus on humanity rather than Christ, are quickly adopting the mantra of the Pope and the UN. After all, what harmonizes better with their message of "hope" and everything getter better than the quest for "world peace?" What better incubator for a Kingdom mentality and utopia than a humanitarian compassion for the poor and needy and an end to all war? Wouldn't that pave the way for their rise to power, and the eventual return of Christ? Perhaps you think all this is far-fetched? Not at all! Common causes often create strange bedfellows. Consider for a moment the following quotes:

"Today is the World Day of Peace, "No longer slaves, but brothers and sisters": this is the message of this day. Because war always makes slaves of us! It is a message that involves all of us. We are all called to combat every form of slavery and to build fraternity -- all of us, each one according to his or her own responsibility. Remember well: peace is possible! And at the root of peace, there is always prayer. Let us pray for peace. There are also good schools of peace, schools for peace: we must go forward with this education of peace."[190]

---

[190] Pope Francis, 1/1/15

"One of the signs of the end times is that people don't train for war. So when people are saying there will be 'wars and rumors of wars,' in the end times they must recognize that we've had that already. We haven't come to the end of our days because not every prophecy is fulfilled. We're still waiting to see a world without wars." [191]

"Let us implore from on high the gift of commitment to the cause of peace. Peace in our homes, our families, our schools and our communities. Peace in all those places where war never seems to end. Peace for those faces which have known nothing but pain. Peace throughout this world which God has given us as the home of all and a home for all. Simply PEACE."[192]

"I'm aware that many don't believe it, but unbiased analysis and a multitude of relevant statistics confirm that the world is actually getting better. There is greater prosperity, peace, and health than ever before in recorded history. The Kingdom of God is boldly advancing and it's transforming everything in its wake."[193]

"God of peace, bring your peace to our violent world: peace in the hearts of all men and women and peace among the nations of the Earth."[194]

World peace is the mission of this Pope, just as it was his predecessors. It is also the mission of the UN and the EU. It is now becoming the focus of the NAR Preterists and Dominionists, with their new gospel of social transformation and social justice. All these groups are convinced that the epicenter of conflict is the Holy Land. Thus, a peace treaty with Israel and

---

[191] *Is It the End of The World as We Know It?* by Kris Vallotton, December 5, 2016

[192] Pope Francis, 9/25/15, Interreligious

[193] "Why You've Been Duped Into Believing the Myth That the World is Getting Worse and Worse," Posted 18th August 2015 by J.D. King, World Revival Network BlogSpot

[194] Pope Benedict XVI

the Palestinians will represent the fulfillment of their dreams. And though they have different motives, they will rally together for the same agenda. All the streams will flow into the same river. They will align together for the cause of "peace and security." They will sit down together at the same table with Israel and the future Antichrist. But before long, their great breakthrough will become their greatest nightmare, and there will be no escape.

All Roads Lead to Rome

The Catholic Popes have been working for unity among Christians for many years. The Vatican has championed the Ecumenical movement, which began in the mid-20ᵗʰ Century. The World Council of Churches (WCC) was formed in 1948, the same year Israel became a nation once again, and partners with the Vatican around the world. Rome sees herself as the "Mother Church" and has always viewed Protestants as "separated brethren." However, the Vatican is not only spearheading unity among "Christians," but has also been actively campaigning for unity among world religions. Much of this was begun by John Paul II, and has heated up enormously under Pope Francis, who has considerably broadened the tent. Indeed, the day after he took office, he met with leaders from ever major religion including Orthodox Christians, Protestant Christian denominations, Jews, Muslims, Buddhists, Sikhs, Hindus, and Jainists. Pope Francis addressed the Muslims first, whom he said, "adore the one, living, and merciful God and who call upon Him in prayer." Then speaking to the general audience, he said:

"The Catholic Church is aware of the importance of the promotion of friendship and respect between men and women of different religious traditions. I want to repeat this: The

promotion of friendship and respect between men and women of different religious traditions."[195]

This was not the first time a Catholic Pope has met with such a body. An inter-faith summit for peace was convened by John Paul II in 1986, in the Italian town of Assisi (home of St Francis), and has continued ever since, being accelerated by Pope Francis. In June 2014, the Pope did something unprecedented, when he brought together Muslims, Jews, Catholics and Orthodox Christians to pray for peace in the Middle East. In the Vatican Garden, he hosted a meeting attended by the former President of Israel, Shimon Peres, Mahmoud Abbas of the Palestinian Authority and Bartholomew I, the Orthodox Patriarch. Prayers were delivered in Italian, Hebrew, Arabic and English, and the Koran was read in the Vatican for the very first time.

Just a few days after that event, Pope Francis welcomed to the Vatican Joel Osteen, a Mormon senator, and a pastor from California. Osteen had this to say after the meeting.

"I like the fact that this pope is trying to make the Church larger, not smaller. He's not pushing people out but making the Church more inclusive. That resonated with me."[196]

Two weeks later, Pope Francis had lunch with another delegation of Charismatics and Evangelicals at the Vatican. The meeting included Kenneth Copeland, James Robison, Geoff Tunnicliffe of Worldwide Evangelical Alliance and others. The participants came away with glowing reports.

---

[195] Pope Francis
[196] *Osteen meets with Pope Francis at Vatican*, by Carol Christian, *Houston Chronicle*, June 6, 2014

"In his written statement released after the Papal meeting, Mr. Robison said he was 'blessed to be part of perhaps an unprecedented moment between evangelicals and the Catholic Pope.' He described the Protestant delegation's private meeting with the leader of the Roman Catholic Church as 'an intimate circle of prayerful discussion and lunch to discuss not only seeing Jesus' prayer answered, but that every believer would become a bold, joy-filled witnesses for Christ.' In describing the ecumenical gathering as a miracle, Mr. Robison said, 'This is something God has done. God wants his arms around the world. And he wants Christians to put his arms around the world by working together.'[197]

From what I have read, it seems all the participants came away with such a "good feeling" about the Pontiff. They all said how humble he was, and how much he "loved Jesus." Shortly after this meeting, I, along with the pastors in the movement that I was part of, received a letter about the event. On the top of the page was a picture of the Pope and the pastors who met with him, and written across it was the phrase, "Unity in Diversity." In this letter, we were being lectured by some young millennial who had obviously not grown up with the Catholic Church. The letter appeared as an article in Revival Magazine.

"This initiative by Pope Francis is a further reaching out to the Evangelical world after his cell phone message recorded earlier this year. This time it is followed up by bringing the five ministry leaders who represent a large portion (in total approx. 900 Million Evangelicals) of the body together for a historical event, which is undeniably God-orchestrated. At the age of 77, Pope Francis is full of strength, bold, outgoing, a people's person, charismatic, and Spirit-filled. Weekly, tens of thousands

---

[197] Pope Francis Meets Evangelical Delegation, Rick Wiles, Canada Free Press

of people flock to St. Peter's Square on Wednesday mornings to hear him share. People are drawn into experiencing the fullness of being a Christian through a daily relationship with Jesus as their Saviour and Lord. He has the potential of being one of the greatest evangelists of the Gospel today! One of the pivotal reasons of today's meeting was to start a conversation together in what it means to receive SALVATION personally. This was the beginning of a Joint Declaration between this large faction of the Evangelical world and the Roman Catholic Church."[198]

There is nothing wrong with meeting the Pope. However, this was more than just a meeting. It was a sell-out of the Christian Church. There was a clear intent and agenda to this gathering, and apparently, a declaration of agreement that we are all one, and "Luther's protest is over." We are told that doctrine or theological beliefs are our diversity -- a blessing in disguise.

"After Vatican Council II, Evangelicals were referred to as "separated brethren" and the idea of this separation in light of ecumenism took on a more cordial form with a term used by Pope John Paul II as 'Organic Unity'.... What we have today with Pope Francis is a term called 'Reconciled Diversity'.... Reconciled Diversity means a "Unity In Diversity" without compromise. Therefore, it is possible to create a Joint Declaration for the purpose of Faith and Mission. The five ministries' leaders, as seen in the photos above and below, will together proclaim and affirm the pre-existing article on the 'Joint Declaration on the Doctrine of Justification'.... There is much more to all this -- the leaders presented Pope Francis concrete ways forward in his initiative by presenting him their written intention of a Joint Declaration, similar to that of the

---

[198] *Unity in Diversity*, by Bruno Ierullo, Jun 25th, 2014, *Revival Magazine*
http://revivalmag.com/article/unity-diversity

Lutheran Church. There is mention in the intent that it would be great joy to celebrate 2017 with an act of Reconciliation. The delegation intend to commit themselves to mutual love and fraternal fellowship while embracing each other's unique diversities, and recognizing their common commitment to the core of the Christian faith, while not minimizing each other's distinctive gifts…. The most exciting part is the commitment to Unity of Faith and Mission, and it will be a miracle to stand united in essential Christian beliefs, while expressing them in varied forms, so that we can evangelize together and cooperate as disciples of Christ in visible unity, for the well-being of all Humanity, so that the World will believe that the Father sent His Son!"[199] (Emphasis Mine)

Another meeting took place with Revival leaders (all in the NAR) in June 2016. The group included Che Ahn, Mike Bickle, Kris Vallotton, and Stacey Campbell. We are told the participants were there to engage in ongoing dialogue. Kris Vallotton had much to say in his blog about the meeting.

"This week I had the privilege of meeting with Pope Francis. It was probably one of the highlights of my life. He was funny, warm and very spiritual. I was invited, along with several other pastors, to a small connect forum with Pope Francis because he has a deep passion for unity among Believers – and I do mean DEEP!....... We spent about two hours asking him questions about whatever was on our hearts. His opening comments blessed me. He said, 'We must invite the prophets back into the Church and welcome them with open arms.' I thought it was interesting that this was his opening comment. Of course, many

[199] *Unity in Diversity*, by Bruno Ierullo, Jun 25th, 2014, *Revival Magazine*
http://revivalmag.com/article/unity-diversity

of the pastors looked over and smiled at me."[200] (Emphasis Mine)

Mr. Vallotton and his friends obviously loved this comment, missing of course, the "back into the Church" part, which underscores their complete ignorance of Catholicism. He goes on:

"Mike Bickle gets the 'guts' award! Everything was going quite smoothly, partly because of the benign questions the pastors were asking. Then Mike stood up and asked the Pope if he believed that Jesus was the 'only way' to heaven. (There have been rumors circulating that Pope Francis is a Universalist). The tension instantly rose in the room...the moderator was noticeably shaken. But the Holy Father didn't blink an eye. He answered, 'We might be surprised by who we meet in heaven. BUT the only way into heaven is through Jesus Christ. There is no other way into heaven.' We all breathed a sigh of relief!"[201]

They all breathed a sigh of relief. Can you imagine! Those rumors about the Pope being a Universalist are just garbage. Really? How incredibly foolish! While I applaud Mike Bickle for asking the question, I am shocked by his naiveté. What did he expect the Pope to say, and in front of all those Christians? "Well, Jesus is just another path." Of course not, the man is the leader of the Roman Catholic Church. That's not Roman Catholic doctrine, and besides, it would have turned off all his guests and ended his hope of reconciliation. With all due respect to these leaders, they are not just showing their ignorance of Catholicism, but also how easily they are beguiled. However, those of us who know Catholicism, and especially the Papacy, understand that nothing is that simple. While the Pope answers

---

[200] *Kris Vallotton Blog, http://krisvallotton.com/pope-francis/*
[201] *Kris Vallotton Blog, http://krisvallotton.com/pope-francis*

the question favorably, he will walk it back in a matter of hours, when it suits the audience that he is addressing. This does not mean that he is necessarily lying, it's just that the Catholic view of Christ, the Church, and the world is a lot more complicated than that of Vallotton or Bickle. Let me present it in the simplistic view of a new "Millennial" leader, one of those who feel they are smarter than everyone who has gone before.

"Multiple Christian leaders who I love and respect who have spent time with him and can tell that he loves Jesus like crazy. And with that love, he is changing the world. I know... there are many things I do differently from Pope Francis (and the rest of the Catholic family). I do church, they do mass. I confess on Facebook, they confess in booth. I baptize old, they baptize new. I do jeans, they do robes. But in all the differences of look and style and tradition, we both preach Christ, and Him crucified."[202]

What these gentlemen don't seem to understand is that their "Johnny Come Lately" practices have no sway on the institution of the Catholic Church. The Pope invited them, and he did not do it in ignorance of who they are and what they represent. They are separated brethren to him and he wants them to come into alignment. I am not suggesting that the Pope is not a very nice man, and that he doesn't love Jesus, but one does not get to be Pope simply by being a nice Christian man. There are many things that the Pope must believe and practice before he is chosen for such a role, like the fact that he is infallible when he speaks on matters of doctrine. Let's be serious here. While he may be "crazy for Jesus" he is also crazy for Mary and has dedicated his life to the Queen of Heaven, as did all his predecessors.

---

[202] *The Awful (And Beautiful) Truth About Pope Francis,* by Carlos A. Rodríguez, http://www.happysonship.com

"This devotion had a profound impact on the devotional life of Pope Francis. As archbishop of Buenos Aires, he introduced and encouraged the devotion to Our Lady, Undoer of Knots. The devotion was so intensely popular throughout Argentina and Brazil that the British Guardian called it "a religious craze."[203]

"Twelve hours after his election as the 266th successor of St. Peter, Pope Francis made a quiet visit to the Basilica of St. Mary Major to venerate the famous icon of Our Lady known as Salus Populi Romani (protectress of the Roman people). The Holy Father placed a small bouquet of flowers before the icon and sang the Salve Regina. Cardinal Abril y Castelló, the archpriest of St. Mary Major, explained the significance of the Holy Father's veneration:

"He decided to visit the basilica, not only to thank the Blessed Virgin, but -- as Pope Francis said to me himself -- to entrust her with his pontificate, to lay it at her feet. Being deeply devoted to Mary, Pope Francis came here to ask her for help and protection."[204]

When the "Holy Father" prays, it's a tad different than just the clothes he wears. We are told he says the Rosary three times a day. Does Mr. Rodríguez know what the Rosary is? Does Mr. Vallotton find that charming also? It takes close to an hour to "say" the Rosary, unless one can repeat each prayer with unusual speed. That's close to three hours a day praying to Mary. Now I realize that Mr. Bickle and his companions have been told by the Catholic hierarchy that they don't worship Mary or the saints. But that is totally false. Of course they do! The

---

[203] *Why does Pope Francis have a special devotion to Our Lady, Undoer of Knots?*
http://catholicstraightanswers.com/why-does-pope-francis-have-a-special-devotion-to-our-lady-undoer-of-knots/
[204] *Why Does Pope Francis Love the Blessed Virgin Mary So Much?* by Deacon Nick Donnelly, *National Catholic Register*

hierarchy has always denied this, in the same way they deny they preach a gospel of works – but they do! Do these dear brothers not know that Roman Catholic belief or practice has not changed that much since the time of Luther? One can still buy an indulgence, a Mass Card (to have a Mass said), or light a candle for one's loved one to get out of purgatory. When one buys a candle and lights it before a statue, or brings a bouquet of flowers and puts it before a statue, and then kneels and prays to the statue, does that not constitute worship? What would the prophet Jeremiah say?

"Do you not see what they are doing in the cities of Judah and in the streets of Jerusalem? The children gather wood, and the fathers kindle the fire, and the women knead dough to make cakes for the queen of heaven; and they pour out drink offerings to other gods in order to spite Me." Jer 7:17-18

The Rosary is essentially a litany to Mary, who is hailed as the Queen of Heaven. There are 50 Hail Mary prayers in the rosary, and at the end of every rosary the Hail Holy Queen is recited. Here is a sample of the Hail Holy Queen:

"Hail, Holy Queen, Mother of Mercy, our life, our sweetness and our hope! To thee do we cry, poor banished children of Eve. To thee do we send up our sighs, mourning and weeping in this valley of tears! Turn, then, O most gracious Advocate, thine eyes of mercy toward us, and after this, our exile, show unto us the blessed fruit of thy womb, Jesus. O clement, O loving, O sweet Virgin Mary." [205]

For those of you who still doubt that RC's worship Mary, consider just this snippet of the litany to Mary prayer.

---

[205] Standard Roman Catholic prayer, Hail Holy Queen

Holy Mary, pray for us.
Holy Mother of God,
Holy Virgin of virgins,
Mother of Christ,
Mother of the Church,
Mother of divine grace,
Mother most pure,
Mother most chaste,
Mother inviolate,
Mother undefiled,
Mother immaculate,

Virgin most powerful,
Virgin most merciful,
Virgin most faithful,
Mirror of justice,
Seat of wisdom,
Cause of our joy,
Spiritual vessel,
Vessel of honor,

Queen of angels,
Queen of patriarchs,
Queen of prophets,
Queen of apostles,
Queen of martyrs,
Queen of confessors,
Queen of virgins,
Queen of all saints,
Queen conceived without original sin,
Queen assumed into heaven,
Queen of the most holy rosary,

Let's be clear! To those Christian pastors who are so enamored by Pope Francis and his love for Jesus, you need to be a bit more discerning. There is a good reason why God raised up the Reformation. But it's not just about worshiping Mary and the saints. There are many other problems as well. There are issues with salvation (which for RC's is both faith and works), issues with the priesthood, issues with indulgences, issues with the infallibility of the Pope, the Assumption and sinlessness of Mary, confession, and the sacrifice of the Mass, just to name a few. Furthermore, though there are many Roman Catholics who have come to know Christ, the vast majority of the 1.2 billion on earth are lost. They were baptized as infants and think they are going to heaven, even though they have never known Christ or walked with Him. Thus, it is complete deception to tell Christians that we are in the same "family." But Kris Valotton, and apparently, Mike Bickle, see no problem with this "reconciled diversity." Indeed, they are aligning themselves with it and appear willing to sign or have signed this "Joint Declaration on the Doctrine of Justification." This should not surprise us, since the NAR has already made it clear that alignment is more important than doctrine or theology. And of course, the Pope is quite comfortable with this. After all, they are the ones that are aligning with him.

"Pope Francis said, 'Theology is a very complicated subject and we should let the theologians argue it out (figure it out). In the meantime, we should love each other and learn to value people who are different than ourselves.' He made it clear that theology shouldn't divide us. I also think he was making a point that he wasn't a theologian, in that he said "they" should work it out while "we" love people."[206]

---

[206] Kris Vallotton Blog, http://krisvallotton.com/pope-francis

Doesn't that sound so refreshing? Can you hear them talking and laughing? "Let's just love people and love one another, and let someone else sort out what we believe! After all, it doesn't matter that much, does it? Don't look at any more books! Don't read what I said on the internet! Don't study the Bible and compare it with what I believe. We are friends now! I love Jesus and you love Jesus and that's all that matters." Now the rest of us who weren't there, didn't walk the red carpet or feel the "presence of God" in the room, are tuned out. We are just religious, old fashioned, doom and gloom Protestants who are holding everyone back from the Kingdom. We are what's wrong with the Church, and now we are the ones breaking such holy unity. It seems though that we are in good company, since the great Apostle Paul warned us of something just like this.

"But even if we, or an angel from heaven, should preach to you a gospel contrary to what we have preached to you, he is to be accursed! As we have said before, so I say again now, if any man is preaching to you a gospel contrary to what you received, he is to be accursed!" Gal 1:8-9 (Emphasis Mine)

Here we are warned that if even Paul himself, or an angel from heaven above, should come with a different gospel other than the one proclaimed to us in Scripture, we are not only to reject it, but to consider the one bringing it accursed. For five centuries Protestant Christians have found the teachings of the Roman Catholic Church incompatible with Scripture, but now all that is brushed aside. We have a much smarter and more loving generation which regrets that approach, and considers relationship and trust a better guide to truth and the will of God. You may remember that the new apostles have sorted all that out.

"In apostleships, the priority of relationships is kept above doctrinal agreement, promoting highly relational core connections. Apostles create covenantal, family relationships, because believers are attached to and through fathers and family, not doctrine. This promotes freedom for people to think creatively, to dream, to envision with God and to experience new depths of the Holy Spirit. This relational security creates an environment that attracts revelation. The very nature of revelation is that people get fresh perspectives and deeper insights with the supernatural kingdom of God."[207]

As we already discovered, the apostles of the NAR no longer need theology for unity or direction. All they need is the two R's, Relationship and Revelation. Their apostolic alignment gives them the security they need to grow and dream. Therefore, it is not hard to understand why they are cozying up to the Pope. But is this really a quest for true Christian unity, or merely an infatuation brought on by their desire for apostolic stature? In any event, it seems clear they have become mesmerized by this potential alliance and have aggressively begun to sell it to their followers.

"We can gain some great insight by contrasting the Protestant movement with the Catholic Church, who is the mother of the Church. In fact, let's do a little trivia: How many times has the Catholic Church split over the last 2000 years? The right answer is three times! How many times has the Protestant Church split since the reformation? Okay, I will make the question easier: How many times has the Protestant Church split this month? Okay, one more question: What does the Catholic Church call the leaders of their local churches? The right answer is father! Are you gaining any insight yet? The apostle Paul put it this way:

---

[207] *Heavy Rain: How to Flood Your World with God's Transforming Power,* by Kris Vallotton

"For if you were to have countless tutors in Christ, yet you would not have any fathers, for in Christ Jesus I became your father through the gospel" (1 Corinthians 4:15). In the 1960s, the Catholic priests preached their messages in Latin! I think it's pretty easy to see that Catholics didn't come to church to hear a great message, because many of them probably didn't even understand the language. As Protestants, we understand the disadvantages of not preaching the Word, and I appreciate that. But why do Catholics go to church? I would like to propose to you that they don't gather because they agree but because they are loyal to a family. Is it possible that when Protestants protested bad doctrine at the price of relationship, we came under another curse just as destructive? (Something to think about.) [208] *(Emphasis Mine)*

There is much to think about in this passage and a good deal more to forget. As much as I appreciate and practice the concept of spiritual fatherhood, and wholeheartedly agree that it is at the core of apostleship, it is hardly comparable to the Roman Catholic priesthood. Mr. Vallotton, in his determination to prove that spiritual fatherhood trumps Biblical truth, has made a monstrous mistake by assuming Roman Catholics view the Church world as Protestants do. Nothing could be further from the truth. After growing up a Catholic, I can assure you that relationship with the priest is not like spiritual fatherhood. Also, I can confirm that most Catholics, if they go to church at all, have no relationship with the priest, and see his interaction with them as purely religious ceremony. The ones who go to church regularly (a small remnant today) do so because they love God, and want to be near Him. The particular priest or church matters little to them, although a friendly one helps. Nevertheless, the vast majority of Catholics throughout the world will go to the

---

[208] *Heavy Rain: How to Flood Your World with God's Transforming Power*, by Kris Vallotton

church closest to them, at the time most convenient for them, and for the least amount of time possible. They are happy just to stand inside the church and "get mass," believing this to fulfill their obligation to God. It appears Mr. Valotton and his friends know very little about Roman Catholicism.

Is the Pope a Universalist?

If we accept Pope Francis' answer to Mike Bickle, then I suppose we would have to say he is not a Universalist. However, that's only one statement to a certain audience. To answer the question, one must consider the entirety of his teaching, and that of the Roman Catholic hierarchy. Another point we must consider is that it is not unusual for the Catholic Pontiff to have a dichotomy of beliefs. They do not view the world like many Protestant leaders. In other words, they are not guided by Scripture in the same way we try to be. For them, "Holy Mother the Church" makes the rules and determines what is correct teaching and doctrine, and that is often contradictory. For instance, the Church teaches that salvation is by faith in what Christ has done, while at the same time it teaches that one can earn God's approval through penitence, indulgences, and special prayers and masses. To us who follow the Bible, these are contradictory, but to them they are in harmony because it is church tradition. In other words, their devotion is not to the teaching of the Bible, but to the institution of the Catholic Church, and sometimes special orders within the Church, such as the Jesuits or the Carmelites, etc. When a person comes to know the Lord as a Catholic, and then begins to study the Bible, they will either leave the Church, or go back to Church teaching, since the Bible and Church teaching are incompatible. Furthermore, the Catholic hierarchy doesn't examine Church teaching to make sure it is Biblical. In fact, church teaching is on the same plane as Scripture and generally supersedes it, since the Pope can change or add to Church teaching anytime he wants to. Remember, he is infallible on these matters.

For many years now, the teaching of the popes and the cardinals has been a mixture of Christianity and humanism. For the faithful, it is mass and the sacraments, but when they give homilies it is all about peace and harmony and good works. They speak of caring for the human family, and how we are all God's children, and how we must all get along, and so on. The encouragement to care for the poor and all that is noble, but it is not the gospel of Christ. Pope Francis has taken this emphasis to new levels. His message is simply world socialism, with open borders, redistribution of wealth, and an alliance of world religions for world peace. He is working feverishly to bring "Christians" together as well as to unite world religions under this umbrella. Each month he releases a video to this end. Let us consider the message from the Pope's video released in January of 2016.

"The Vatican releases an extremely disturbing video in which Pope Francis declared that all of the major world religions are 'seeking God or meeting God in different ways' and that ultimately 'we are all children of God.' The video also featured leaders from various major religions, and they are shown declaring fidelity to their particular gods. First, we see a female Buddhist cleric tell us 'I have confidence in the Buddha,' followed by a Jewish rabbi declaring 'I believe in God.' As the video goes on, a Catholic priest announces 'I believe in Jesus Christ,' and last of all an Islamic leader boldly declares 'I believe in God, Allah.' After watching that video, nobody can deny that the Vatican is openly promoting a one world religion."[209] *(Emphasis Mine)*

---

[209] *12 Times Pope Francis Has Openly Promoted a One World Religion or a New World Order*, Michael Snyder, 8/1/2016
https://www.youtube.com/watch?v=-6FfTxwTX34

The Harlot Church

The book of Revelation, despite the Preterist claims, was written by John while exiled to the Isle of Patmos around the year 95AD. We have significant testimony to this fact from inside the book itself,[210] and from the Early Church fathers.[211] The Revelation concerns the time of the Day of the Lord, or the 3 ½ year Tribulation period at the end of the age. To understand the book, it is necessary to have a background in the Hebrew Prophets, since much of it is a repeat of their testimony concerning the Day of the Lord. For instance, chapters 13, 17 and 18 directly correlate with the book of Daniel, chapters 2, 7, and 8. For a more complete review of this topic, please see my book *The 7 Lost Keys of End-Time Prophecy.*[212]

In chapter 13, two beasts are mentioned. The first one represents the political system under Antichrist, and the second one represents a religious system under a false prophet.

"Then I saw another beast coming up out of the earth; and he had two horns like a lamb and he spoke as a dragon. He exercises all the authority of the first beast in his presence. And he makes the earth and those who dwell in it to worship the first beast, whose fatal wound was healed. He performs great signs, so that he even makes fire come down out of heaven to the earth in the presence of men. And he deceives those who dwell on the earth because of the signs which it was given him to perform in the presence of the beast, telling those who dwell on

---

[210] It's origin in the province of Asia at a time of severe oppression of Christians, which is most conceivable under Domitian

[211] "We will not, however, incur the risk of pronouncing positively as to the name of Antichrist; for if it were necessary that his name should be distinctly revealed in this present time, it would have been announced by him who beheld the apocalyptic vision. For it was seen not very long time since, but almost in our day, towards the end of Domitian's reign." Iraneus, Against Heresies, 30

[212] *The 7 Lost Keys of End-Time Prophecy,"* by PJ Hanley, available at Amazon.com

the earth to make an image to the beast who had the wound of the sword and has come to life." Rev 13:11-14

The fact that the beast had two horns like a lamb and spoke as a dragon is a picture of a false prophet. It is reminiscent of how Jesus compared false prophets to wolves in sheep's clothing. Notice how this false prophet, representing a religious system, performs great signs and turns the world toward the Antichrist. More information is given on the identity of this false prophet in chapter 17. John receives a vision of a woman riding a beast with 7 heads and 10 horns. Without getting into too much detail on the beast, we know from Daniel that it represents the last kingdom under Antichrist. For this discussion, however, we will focus on the woman that rides the political system.

"And he carried me away in the Spirit into a wilderness; and I saw a woman sitting on a scarlet beast, full of blasphemous names, having seven heads and ten horns. The woman was clothed in purple and scarlet, and adorned with gold and precious stones and pearls, having in her hand a gold cup full of abominations and of the unclean things of her immorality, and on her forehead a name was written, a mystery, 'BABYLON THE GREAT, THE MOTHER OF HARLOTS AND OF THE ABOMINATIONS OF THE EARTH.' And I saw the woman drunk with the blood of the saints, and with the blood of the witnesses of Jesus. When I saw her, I wondered greatly. And the angel said to me, 'Why do you wonder? I will tell you the mystery of the woman and of the beast that carries her, which has the seven heads and the ten horns.'" Rev 17:3-7

There has been, and continues to be, much speculation on the identity of the woman, or "Mystery Babylon," as many refer to her. Indeed, a new book has just been written contending it is in fact Jerusalem, and this by a Premillennialist. However, this is nonsense and completely unnecessary, since the chapter itself gives the identity of the woman.

"The woman whom you saw is the great city, which reigns over the kings of the earth." Rev 17:18

There is only one city that fits that description, not only at the time of the writing, but throughout the whole of the 1st Century. The ancient city of Babylon was in ruins, and Jerusalem was certainly not reigning over the kings of the earth. Thus, the identity of the woman is Rome. This is not speculation, but plain fact. Now let us add to this knowledge the rest of the detail on the woman from the chapter.

1. The woman is said to be a harlot. This is spiritual language depicting unfaithfulness to the Lord. This understanding is clear from many passages in the Prophets, as well as the teaching of the Lord Himself, who referred to the faithful as virgins.

2. The woman is not the beast but rides on top of the beast. This means that at the End-Time she is not the political system itself but is brought to power by it and is allied with it. The beast appears at the end of the age, and the woman, Rome, rides on the political kingdom of the Antichrist. Thus, Rome is not necessarily the capital of the Antichrist.

3. She has a history of persecuting the true Church and the Jews, since she is full of the blood of the saints.

4. Her colors are purple and scarlet and she has a gold cup in her hand which is full of abominations.

5. This religious city of Rome is destroyed by the Antichrist toward the end of the Tribulation.

"And he said to me, 'The waters which you saw where the harlot sits, are peoples and multitudes and nations and tongues. And the ten horns which you saw, and the beast, these will hate the harlot and will make her desolate and naked, and will eat her flesh and will burn her up with fire.'" Rev 17:15-16

If you followed all that, then you already know the identity of the woman. It is the city of Rome that appears again at the end of the age, with a religious connotation, and in close alliance with the political system of the Antichrist. All the terminology fits perfectly with the Roman Catholic Church. The Pope will be the head of this harlot Church alliance, and an alliance of world religions. He will be the false prophet that works alongside the Antichrist and convinces the world to worship him. The present pope is following this scenario to a tee, however his age suggests his successor may be the one. Nevertheless, it is abundantly clear that the office of the Roman Pontiff is tailor-made to fulfill these prophecies. It is also clear that this office is leading a harlot Church and will unite all religions under it for the cause of humanism and world peace. And now sadly we know that this alliance will also include the NAR apostles who will lead a large contingent of Charismatics, Pentecostals, Evangelicals and Revival Churches into it. Because they were already deceived, they will fall for the ultimate deception. Because they put relationship and alignment above God's word, they will be enticed into the ultimate alignment. They will plot together against Israel and the true Bride of Christ. And once the deed is done and the Antichrist is revealed, many will come to their senses, but they will have missed the Rapture, and will suffer brutally during the Tribulation period.

Conclusion
Unity among Christians is something to be pursued and protected. All genuine believers want to share unity with one

another. However, we can only have unity with those who are in Christ and who have Christ in them. Paul told us to preserve the unity of the Spirit in the bond of peace.[213] It is assumed that if we are in Christ, and have His Spirit in us, we will already have this unity, and should do everything possible to preserve it. There is another unity spoken about in the same passage, and that is the unity of the faith.[214] This unity has to do with a common understanding and agreement concerning the Word of God, and the faith once and for all delivered to the saints. It is possible, of course, to have relational unity with someone from another denomination or church who has received the Holy Spirit as we have. However, if we are to have any kind of functional unity, there must be unity of the faith. In other words, we need to be on the same page regarding the essential teaching of the Word of God. Those Christian leaders who reject the need for doctrinal agreement and forge ahead with a unity based on feelings, or relationship alone, are undermining the Word of God and misleading the Body of Christ. What they end up with is not true Christian unity, but an alliance built on compromise and man's agenda. It is better to be Christ-like toward each other, while challenging errant theology, than to sweep it under the rug for unity's sake. The fruit of such unions is always bad.

The Bible is clear that the end of the age will be a time of alliances. We are told that the Antichrist Empire will be an alliance of nations that come together for a specific purpose, rather than a cohesive monarchy.[215] The same appears to be true for the religious system that is described as the Harlot, who rides the beast. It is an alliance, or alignment, for a specific purpose that is presented as noble and even Christian, but in reality, it is

---

[213] Eph 4:3
[214] Eph 4:13
[215] Dan 2:42-43, Rev 17:12-13

war against God Himself. Those who push truth aside for so-called "apostolic" alignment now are preparing themselves and their networks for the ultimate alignment with the Apostolic See (Vatican). Their thirst for dominion will cause them to be bewitched. Their decreeing of worldwide revival opens them to deception, unreality, and false visions. Their desire to be recognized and lauded as apostles attracts them to the red carpet. And their "happily ever after" view of the End-Times guarantees them a seat next to the Antichrist to participate in the apostasy of the ages!

"I heard another voice from heaven, saying, "Come out of her, my people, so that you will not participate in her sins and receive of her plagues; for her sins have piled up as high as heaven, and God has remembered her iniquities." Rev 18:4-5

Chapter Nine
Saving the Baby & Losing the Bathwater
The Bridal Remnant

If you have managed to read this book, you have acquired some very necessary information. You may also have become troubled by these discoveries. I remember when I first began to uncover the existence of the NAR and its influence within the movement of which I was a part. I was shattered! I felt betrayed! How could these dear friends of mine that I looked up to sell us out? How could they place us all under other leaders without our consent? How could they be part of something so secretive, and so doctrinally contradictory to where we were? I was deeply troubled. And the more I discovered the more I became ill. I kept feeling a sense of alarm, but it seemed nobody either knew or cared. I wrestled with my feelings before God daily. I didn't know what to do. It would have been easier to just say nothing, and ride along, but I couldn't. Once I saw the direction it was all going, how could I be silent? I knew I would be rejected and marginalized, and I was, but what other options were there? We took our church out, worked through forgiveness and moved on. Perhaps you find yourself in the same place and don't know what to do. Maybe your church is caught up in all this stuff, or maybe you are, and you are the pastor? What do you do now? That is the purpose of this chapter -- to help us all get back on track with what God is doing in these Last Days.

The title of this chapter may seem a bit strange to you, particularly if you are a Millennial. It is an old saying, and one that has been used a lot by Charismatics. It comes from the time when folks did not have fancy bathtubs, but only tubs and basins to wash their babies in. At the end of the wash, the water was thrown outside. Thus, the warning, "Don't throw the baby out with the bathwater." This is quite easy to do, although not with actual babies. However, the idea is that we can become so disgusted with the dirty water that we forget there is something valuable in it, and throw it out also. It happens all the time. We become so repulsed by what is wrong, what is off, that we dismiss everything. In the last eight chapters, we have discussed the dirty water of the current Apostolic Movement. If you have seen the slime and smelled the smell, you are already starting to throw it from you. However, let's be careful to get rid of the dirty water only, while we hold on to what has been given by God Himself.

Forgiveness

Perhaps the material in this book has presented a crisis for you. Maybe you find yourself feeling angry or betrayed. Somebody once said that trials can make us better or bitter, depending on how we respond. This is absolutely true! For those of us who love Him and want His plan for our lives, God promises to work all things out for our good. What a wonderful promise this is. However, to walk in these promises we must forgive. Jesus warned us that forgiveness was not optional. Indeed, it is absolutely necessary to walk in the grace of God.[216] Therefore, the very first thing you must do is forgive the leaders of the Body of Christ. Also, you must forgive your own pastors or leaders if they have gotten mixed up in it. If you have been betrayed before, or if you have struggled with authority issues, this may be very difficult for you. Nevertheless, if you are going to walk in freedom in your own life you must forgive them from the heart. This does not mean that your angry feelings will all go the first time you do it. You may have to do it repeatedly until your feelings line up with your choice.

---

[216] Mt 18:23-35

Another thing that really helps us to forgive is to pray for the people we are angry with. It is hard to stay angry with someone you are praying for. Pray for them daily if you must and don't pray angry prayers. Pray for God to open their eyes as He has yours. Pray for God to protect them and speak to them. As you choose to forgive and pray for these leaders, you will find your heart changing and being filled with compassion for them. You will begin to understand some of the reasons they got mixed up in all of this. Remember, many of them are unaware of the mess they have gotten into, and they need someone to pray for them. However, in this, do not make them the focus in your heart. You are forgiving them so that you can walk in God's grace. It is imperative that you do this so you can move on and not be derailed by the sins of others.

Another important point that must be made is that if your leaders are into the NAR, and you talk to them, they may not listen to you. In fact, they may even dismiss you and this book, claiming that we are "legalists" and "religious spirits." If that happens, you must still work through forgiveness, even if you feel you need to look for another church to participate in. Whatever you do, do not abandon the Church altogether. That would be a grave mistake. God never intended you to be alone, without other believers in your life. If you try to go it alone, you will certainly backslide since it is not God's will for you. You are part of the Body of Christ and you cannot cut yourself off. So, keep looking for other believers who love God and His Word that you can grow with.

The Why Question
When we deal with trauma, especially in the Church, we sometimes want to know why it all happened. Why would so many Christian leaders go "off the rails" or allow themselves to be hijacked by others calling themselves "apostles?" It is a valid

question. Nevertheless, you must embrace the answer and stop asking the question. God has given us free will. All of us are faced with choices daily that can affect the outcome of our lives. Many of these leaders are being sifted by God in the same way Peter was.[217] We trust that many of them will recover and strengthen the Church in the days ahead. But as to the sifting and testing, remember that God allows all of us to be sifted and tested. It is how we know we love Him more than anything else. All impure motives and attitudes must be removed from His presence. The Bride of Christ must love Him with all her heart, soul, mind and strength. We can have no other lovers before Him. Throughout the ages, believers have been sifted and tested. How much more then, at the end of the age? Jesus warned us that there would be many false prophets and leaders, and so did the Apostles. Why then are we surprised? Is it not merely more proof that we are in the end of the age, and Christ our beloved Bridegroom is coming soon? The great church at Ephesus that was commended by Paul was later admonished by Christ, because they had lost their first love.[218] How did they do that? They got cold. And so can we. Remember, the devil is always prowling around looking for someone to devour. But we are told to resist him firm in the faith. It doesn't say "firm in faith" but "firm in *the* faith." This is the faith once and for all delivered to the saints. It is the gospel of Christ, the Word of God. This is what we are to be firm in and hold onto. Yet many have never become truly grounded in the Word, or as we have seen, have compromised the Word for some influence or stature. Many have fallen into the snare of pride, which is the foundation of the Apostolic Movement. They have gotten their eyes off Jesus, the author and perfecter of *the* faith.[219] Dear Friend, no longer ask why this happened. Ask instead about yourself. What about

---

[217] Luke 22:31-32
[218] Eph 1:15-17, Rev 2:2-5
[219] Heb 12:2

you? Will you take your eyes off Jesus? Will you stand strong in the faith?

The True Apostolic Teaching

"For I am jealous for you with a godly jealousy; for I betrothed you to one husband, that to Christ I might present you as a pure virgin. But I am afraid, lest as the serpent deceived Eve by his craftiness, your minds should be led astray from the simplicity and purity of devotion to Christ." 2 Cor 11:2-3

We have heard the teaching of the "New Apostles" and how they are preoccupied with the Church. We have seen their agenda, and listened as they presented the Church as a commodity, to be marketed and sold to the world. This is the spirit of harlotry. The true apostolic teaching is not Church-centered, nor changing with the seasons of revelation. The Apostles' teaching was and is Christ. We know what they taught because we know what they wrote. The apostolic burden was not about mobilization, but devotion. The Apostle was jealous for God's people with a godly jealousy, that they would belong to no one but Christ, and be preoccupied with no one but Him. His goal was to present them as a pure virgin to the heavenly Bridegroom, and not align them with human leaders. How can we miss this? This man traveled and evangelized the whole world, had more real visions that any modern apostle or prophet, and yet he did not view his mission as equipping the Church to transform culture. He was preparing a virgin, a Bride for the Bridegroom. Indeed, the whole focus of his ministry was Christ. The foundation was Christ, the building was Christ, the alignment was Christ, and they were built up into Christ. How dare anyone fill the minds of God's people with any other vision, any other passion, any other mission than to gain Christ and be with Him.

"Jude, a bond-servant of Jesus Christ, and brother of James, to those who are the called, beloved in God the Father, and kept for Jesus Christ: may mercy and peace and love be multiplied to you." Jude 1-2 (Emphasis Mine)

The Apostles had a holy love for the Church because she belonged to Christ. They were jealous for her that nothing else would become her focus or fancy. They taught the Scriptures, majoring on Christ. They were concerned that the believers would know Him, grow in Him and wait for Him. They confronted false teaching and false teachers that were leading the minds of the believers astray. This is the true apostolic message!

"You therefore, beloved, knowing this beforehand, be on your guard so that you are not carried away by the error of unprincipled men and fall from your own steadfastness, but grow in the grace and knowledge of our Lord and Savior Jesus Christ. To Him be the glory, both now and to the day of eternity. Amen." 2 Pet 3:17-18 (Emphasis Mine)

The Bridal Posture

"FOR THIS REASON A MAN SHALL LEAVE HIS FATHER AND MOTHER AND SHALL BE JOINED TO HIS WIFE, AND THE TWO SHALL BECOME ONE FLESH. This mystery is great; but I am speaking with reference to Christ and the church." Eph 5:31-32

Many in the Church today have completely lost the concept of Bridal love. Indeed, with all the material that we ploughed through in this book, it was not to be found anywhere. The Church seems to be preoccupied with the here and now, and how they can get heaven to bring its goodies here. But the Church is betrothed to Christ. This is not just an analogy to help us preach intimacy and closeness -- it is reality. He is preparing for a wedding and we are waiting to be married.

"Do not let your heart be troubled; believe in God, believe also in Me. In My Father's house are many dwelling places; if it were not so, I would have told you; for I go to prepare a place for you. If I go and prepare a place for you, I will come again and receive you to Myself, that where I am, there you may be also." John 14:1-3

Jesus comforted the Church at that last supper, telling them that He was going to prepare a place for them. In the midst of His sorrow over what was about to happen, He focused Himself on the joy set before Him. He told them that just as surely as He was going away to prepare a place, He would also come back for them that they may be with Him. This He spoke to all of us who are betrothed to Him.

We know that Jesus was speaking in this passage about a Jewish wedding, and that He, as the Bridegroom, was going back to the Father's house to prepare the *Chupah,* or Wedding Chamber.[220] When it is finished to the Father's satisfaction, then Jesus will come again to receive His Bride to Himself, that where He is, she may be also. This was the joy set before Him as He went to the Cross. Yet we are constantly given this picture of Jesus sitting around heaven, waiting and praying for the Church to accomplish this great work of subduing the planet, so He can come again. What a horrible joke! How completely crazy this is? We are told that Jesus is waiting and we are the ones that must do the work, so He won't have to wait anymore. But Jesus said

---

[220] For more on this theme see, *Here Comes the Bride*, by Richard Booker, 1995, Small Booklet

the exact opposite. He is busy preparing a place for us. When it is ready, He will come. The Bridegroom doesn't wait for the Bride. On the contrary, the Bride waits for the Bridegroom, and we are told to wait for Him.[221]

As I write this, I am reminded of my granddaughter who is going to be married in a few months. If you could simply see the excitement on her face. She is scratching off the days, hours and minutes as her wedding approaches. Is she sitting around? No! She's very busy, but I can assure you her attention is focused on her wedding day. The same is true for the Bride of Christ. We are captivated with the wedding and being with Him. He wants so much to be with us. What an apostolic concept. We are busy doing His work, but our hearts are pounding with excitement as we see the day approaching. This is the posture of the Bride.

"If then you have been raised up with Christ, keep seeking the things above, where Christ is, seated at the right hand of God. Set your mind on the things above, not on the things that are on earth. For you have died and your life is hidden with Christ in God. When Christ, who is our life, is revealed, then you also will be revealed with Him in glory." Col 3:1-4 (Emphasis Mine)

We are being told here that our minds are to be set on things above. We are not just thinking about all the nice things in heaven, and how we can bring them to earth. No way! We are focused on Christ, who is our life. We have no other passion, no other obsession, than to be with Him and to be revealed with Him. We are looking up and not down. We are focused on the one who is above and not the things of the earth. Our minds are set on heaven not on the earth and its problems. That isn't the message of the Pope, and it isn't the message of the NAR

---

[221] 1 Thess 1:10

apostles, but it is the message of Scripture, not in one place, but everywhere. Jesus Himself told us that our focus was to be heavenward and not earthly. Seeing the signs of the end of the age we are to look up.

"But when these things begin to take place, straighten up and lift up your heads, because your redemption is drawing near." Luke 21:28

How dare these "apostles" tell us to look down and make life on earth our focus? Who are they? Who authorized them to preach this? Definitely not Jesus. It is no wonder they wanted another apostolic age so they could come up with a new message. This is the message of Jesus and the Apostles, but since they have a new apostolic age, they have come up with a new message. Focus on earth. Focus on the culture. Focus on the 7 Mountains so we can sit as the harlot of Revelation 17. But the Bride of Christ won't listen to that message. Her eyes are fixed on the heavenly Zion of Revelation 14. She follows the Lamb wherever He goes. Being with Him is what she is looking for and living for. And as she sees the day approaching, her heart is beating faster.

"Let us hold fast the confession of our hope without wavering, for He who promised is faithful; and let us consider how to stimulate one another to love and good deeds, not forsaking our own assembling together, as is the habit of some, but encouraging one another; and all the more as you see the day drawing near." Heb 10:23-25

What is this confession of hope that we are holding fast? It is the soon coming of Jesus for His Bride -- the deliverance mentioned in the previous chapter (9:28). This is what we are to encourage one another with. This is what we are to be excited about. And as we can see the day drawing near, because of the signs, we are exhorted to meet more often and confess our great hope to one another. This is the Bridal posture -- looking up, eagerly waiting.

Dear Friends, we have a great hope coming. It is a blessed hope -- an awe-inspiring hope. Our hope is not in man. Our hope is not in the church. How foolish it is to put one's hope in the Church, or apostles or unity. Our hope is in Christ and Him alone. Find yourself a congregation who loves Jesus and the Bible and who have placed their hope in the soon return of Christ.

Saving Souls & Making Disciples

Jesus said that the gospel of His coming Kingdom would be preached in the whole world for a witness, and then the end, or the Kingdom would come.[222] For two thousand years, this word has been fulfilled. The earth has been saturated with the gospel and the end is now very near. Nevertheless, there are people all around us who need to know Jesus. Until the Lord comes for us, and as we wait in eager expectation, we must also be given to His work of making disciples. The NAR apostles and prophets have so corrupted the Great Commission. With their twist of the passage to Christianize nations and transform culture, they have aborted the mission. All the talk and "Kingdom" activity has done little to evangelize and win souls. As we break free from this debilitating influence, let us embrace again the command to make disciples.

"Go therefore and make disciples of all the nations, baptizing them in the name of the Father and the Son and the Holy Spirit,

---

[222] Mt 24:14

teaching them to observe all that I commanded you; and lo, I am with you always, even to the end of the age." Mt 28:19-20

Jesus told us to make disciples of individuals. This involves evangelism and teaching. Therefore, it cannot be accomplished without the local church. Evangelists can help the Church reach people for Christ, but once they are saved they must be discipled. And despite all the talk about "new paradigms" and "new wineskins," history has proven that the best way to make disciples is through local churches. Indeed, the vast majority of those who have come to know the Lord were invited to church by a friend or neighbor. So, let's stop listening to all the hogwash and get back to doing the work of God.

When we consider Jesus' command to teach, we can better understand the Early Church's commitment to the ministry of the Word. Jesus wants converts to be instructed on everything that He commanded. Also, the Church needs to be encouraged regularly, built up in the faith, and trained so that they can do the work. This is, indeed, a lot of teaching. Thus, local churches need not be concerned about too much teaching. We need meetings just to spend time worshipping, and being in God's presence, yet we will always need to teach and preach. Where disciples are being made, there will be a lot of teaching. However, we must teach people the whole counsel of God[223]and not just selected passages or curriculum. It's time to stop thinking that discipleship or ministry training consists of a book on the Father's love, and a class on prophetic activation. Christians need to be taught the whole Bible from cover to cover. There is no excuse. If they are not grounded in this way, they will be shallow, and easily deceived by what sounds good or gives them goosebumps.

---

[223] Acts 20:27

The Church is a Family

"So then you are no longer strangers and aliens, but you are fellow citizens with the saints, and are of God's household (family)..." Eph 2:19 (Parenthesis Mine)

The Church is a family. This is a simple concept, yet it is surprising how many churches and leaders don't grasp it. Every family has parents and so do spiritual families. When the Scripture tells pastors to shepherd God's household, it is telling them to be good parents. Good parents care for their children. They teach them and train them and are happy when they excel. In the same way, godly pastors are spiritual parents to the local church. In this atmosphere of family, wounded people can receive healing from life's hurts, and all can learn and grow. In time, healthy families will produce more healthy families and new local churches will be planted. Thus, healthy local churches are true apostolic centers.

It is also important to remember to hold onto all that the Lord has given us from previous revivals, while we position ourselves for more to come. The power and presence of the Holy Spirit must be the focal point as we learn and live and love together. There is no tension between the Word of God and the Spirit of God. We should be looking for, and experiencing, the power and presence of the Holy Spirit continually, while we teach and preach the Word of God. We must be careful not to overreact to all the false teachers, and heaven chasers, and become knowledge centered rather than Christ centered.

"Be on guard for yourselves and for all the flock, among which the Holy Spirit has made you overseers, to shepherd the church of God which He purchased with His own blood." Acts 20:28

"Therefore, I exhort the elders among you, as your fellow elder and witness of the sufferings of Christ, and a partaker also of the glory that is to be revealed, shepherd the flock of God among you, exercising oversight not under compulsion, but voluntarily, according to the will of God; and not for sordid gain, but with eagerness; nor yet as lording it over those allotted to your charge, but proving to be examples to the flock. And when the Chief Shepherd appears, you will receive the unfading crown of glory." 1 Pet 5:1-4

With all due respect to the NAR Apostolic Centers, the Church of God is not a herd of cattle to be deployed, but a flock of sheep to be cared for. Cattle can be driven but sheep must be led. Godly pastors and apostles will care for the flock of God, knowing they are Christ's special possession, and not a means to an end. All of us who lead God's people are given a sober warning, that they were purchased by His Blood, and must be treated with great love and care. What a great calling it is to be a pastor! What a great responsibility to care for the people of God? Churches are not struggling today because there are too many pastors and not enough apostles. On the contrary, they are languishing because of a shortage of pastors and apostles who have the heart of a true shepherd. Therefore, I want to encourage all those local pastors out there, who are committed to shepherding the Church. You may not be famous; you may not be recognized by the powerful and influential; you may not be selling books or packing conferences, but don't be distracted by all that. Keep doing the great work of God and keep your eyes on the Chief Shepherd who is coming soon to give you your great reward.

What About Networks
After all the discussion of alignment, it is important to address this whole business of networks. Is it a good trend or a bad one?

If there was such a thing as a relational network, then it would not be a network. In other words, if we have real relationships with other leaders, then why would we need to have some organizational structure to hold us together. As we have seen already there are no networks in the Bible. The Twelve Apostles were given a unique ministry, which continues to this day, therefore, there is no need for a replacement. Relationships should be organic and not contrived. If you are worried about accountability, I can assure you that being part of a network is not the answer. One can be part of several networks and yet feel alone. Networking is a secular business model and not a Biblical one. In fact, most networks are hopeless at pastoring or helping people with personal issues. What you are calling a need for accountability, is more likely a desire for friendship and a peer. If you are a pastor and have other local pastor friends, then you are blessed. You can find peer-level friendship, yet be careful not to allow yourself to be compromised. When all is said and done, there is no substitute for a close walk with God. Your alignment needs to be with Jesus, then you will not worry so much about what others do or think. Accountability comes out of character and love for God and His people. True shepherds will not want to hurt God's people by their words or actions. Therefore, they are more likely to surround themselves with safeguards, so they too can be held accountable. When leaders are not walking it out, caring for the Church of God, or teaching sound doctrine, networks, rather than confronting this, often give such leaders a place to hide. And should someone close to that leader, bring a genuine complaint or confrontation, they are usually shot down by the network leaders, who wish to protect the reputation of the network rather than the integrity of the ministry.

If you are an apostolic leader who has mentored others and planted churches, you will continue to be a spiritual parent to them, and a grandparent to their spiritual children. This is good and healthy networking, where the focus is on the work of Christ, in each of the churches, rather than the network itself. Networks must never become the focus. Organization should not go beyond a name and shared theology and values. If it does, then it is only a matter of time before the network will become the focus and the driving force. The second generation of leaders will become less organic and more institutional. However, if we follow the New Testament model, of spiritual fatherhood and true apostolic ministry, then the network will serve the churches, rather than subvert them.

If you are a pastor and your church is part of a network that is aligned with the NAR, then you have a choice to make. There is no doubt that this alignment has become controlling and is leading the Church in the wrong direction. However, the same can be said for most networks and denominations. That is why it is best to avoid them altogether. Should you be part of a network or denomination that is not requiring some sort of "apostolic alignment," and is not setting the direction for your church, then you are wise to carry on and be a source of blessing to them. However, you may find yourself at some point down the road, needing to re-examine your involvement. Whatever you do, do not fall into the trap that some sort of alignment with apostolic networks is necessary. It is not! Align yourself and your church with Jesus, and keep your focus on Him. Build relationships with others organically and get on with the work of Christ. Of course, this will mean that many doors will close to your ministry because of the NAR influence, but others will open and you will be happy serving God and the Last Days Bridal Remnant. Remember, you are not following Christ for recognition in this age, but your reward will come when He does.

Conclusion

For those of us who align ourselves with Christ alone, believe in His soon return, and hold to the authority of Scripture, our most difficult adjustment is accepting the concept of a remnant. We have become so used to the idea of a large global Church, all on the same path, that the reality we now see is quite a shock. Yet, the Bible is clear that in the Last Days many will fall away from the faith, betray one another, and even oppose the Lord Himself. And when He said many, He meant the vast majority. The gate is small and the way is narrow for those who want Christ, and follow Him alone.[224] The Last Days Bride of Christ is a remnant. The global Church, even the one in revival, is posturing itself to play the harlot role in the days ahead. The lines are being drawn now, and the stakes are very high. Deceptive lies and distracting causes are sifting God's people like never before. Therefore, as the wise virgins, we must be prepared, focused, steadfast, and unwavering. The veiled threats that are growing will soon become unveiled. The non-aligned will become the spoilers, the fundamentalists, the extremists that always hinder progress and unity -- the enemies of peace. But what must we do? Run to the hills and hide in bunkers with dehydrated food? No, there is no safe house except God's house, and no security outside the will of God. We are not a lamp to be hidden, or a minority that lives in fear. We are the overcoming Bride that will sit on the Throne with our beloved Bridegroom. What was said of Israel in the Last Days, will first be true of us also. As the darkness increases, so will His glory on us.[225] We will overcome because of the righteousness of Christ (blood of the Lamb), the testimony of God's Word,[226] and a willingness to die for what we believe, if need be. This is

---

[224] Mt 7:13-14

[225] Is 60:1-2

[226] Rev 12:11, The original Greek says "the word of the testimony." This is not just a personal testimony, but the testimony of God's Word, which has also become our testimony. It is the word of the witness, the gospel of Christ which has been preached to the whole world. Mt 24:14

a first fruits, Bridal Company, that through their life and witness, overthrow the kingdom of darkness that is cast from the heavens, and rise to meet the Lord in the air. Yes, indeed, those who endure to the end shall be delivered! Let the Bride now prepare herself.[227] I wish to end this work with a politically incorrect and truly apostolic benediction.

"If anyone does not love the Lord, let him be accursed. Maranatha. The grace of the Lord Jesus be with you. My love be with you all in Christ Jesus. Amen." 1 Cor 16:22-24

---

[227] Rev 19:7

Addendum
NAR Update & Deniers (May 2021)

Since this book was written four years ago more and more people are waking up to the existence of the New Apostolic Reformation or what is commonly called the NAR. Though the structure continues to evolve and morph into different organizations and councils, it is much bigger and now holds a firm grip on the Charismatic church worldwide, together with a large swath of the Pentecostal movement. Much of what I said would happen in this book already has. There is hardly anyone who is known in these circles that is not either a member of, or aligned with, ICAL or USCAL or Wagner University or HIM or Global Spheres or Revival Alliance or Bethel, and on and on it goes. And they are all friends who will never confront anything the other says, because they are either "apostolically aligned" or friends with someone who is. Just read the council member directories and roundtable lists. It's always the same people at the convening table or the leadership councils. And though they are hush hush about their inner circles of apostles and prophets, there is enough information online to figure it out. One cannot just show up to any of these groups. They are by invitation only. And when someone comes along that becomes well known, they will be taken into confidence by one of those leaders who will begin the friendship that leads to alignment, or at least, verbal agreement with the goals of the movement. These goals and boasts continue as before and in some respects have gotten more arrogant. Consider that this statement from Peter Wagner still appears on the ICAL Definition page.

"The Second Apostolic Age began roughly in 2001, heralding the most radical change in the way church is done since the Protestant Reformation. This New Apostolic Reformation embraces the largest segment of non-Catholic Christianity

worldwide and is the fastest growing. Churches of the Apostolic Movement embrace the only Christian mega block growing faster than Islam."[228]

Succession

Chuck Pierce continues to play a key role with his Global Spheres. Consider this statement on his webpage:

"What an honor to have been able to work, serve and walk with Dr. Peter Wagner. Peter was instrumental in helping me form Global Spheres, Inc. as the transitional wineskin for the contacts and associations that had developed through the years, predominantly from our involvement in the world-wide prayer ministry. In 2012, we ended the Global Harvest Ministries wineskin and Global Spheres, Inc. began functioning in a new capacity. Peter served as Vice-President and Ambassadorial Apostle until his home-going in October 2016. Doris, his wonderful lifelong ministry partner, continues to serve as a minister of Global Spheres, Inc. Since the onset of GSI, we have constantly been moving individuals in every sphere from the pastoral, prophetic and intercessory movements into this better defined apostolic wineskin that aligns apostolic, prophetic leaders around the world. To be successful, we need prayer, prophetic revelation, apostolic leadership, and a developed strategy for transformation that will penetrate each molder of culture in a nation with God's Kingdom plan."[229] *Emphasis Mine*

Notice why he says Global Spheres exist – to align people with apostolic and prophetic leaders around the world – his friends. Also, this incredible statement appears on his Glory of Zion page.

---

[228] https://www.icaleaders.com/about-ical/definition-of-apostle
[229] https://globalspheres.org/out page

"Glory of Zion International Ministries is a 'One New Man' ministry that connects people of all nations, backgrounds, races, and walks of life so that we may worship together as one. Ultimately, this is a reflection of God's original intent: the joining of Jew and Gentile together (Eph. 2:15). We desire to support apostolic-prophetic leadership in mobilizing a Kingdom remnant in their cities, provinces and nations. We also long to see Apostolic Centers established from nation to nation. Led by Dr. Charles 'Chuck' D. Pierce, Glory of Zion International expresses the heart and mind of God to individuals, cities, territories and nations, helping them to advance in their own calls."[230] *Emphasis Mine*

Despite this, it is not clear what leadership role Chuck Pierce plays in the movement at this stage. He is definitely one of the top leaders but not the presiding apostle even though the Wagner Baton was passed to him. However, it was also passed to Ché Ahn if you recall, who became the chancellor of the Wagner Institute which is now Wagner University (WU). This arm of the movement seems to be rising to the top since it contains the Revival Alliance, Harvest International Ministries (HIM), and of course Bethel.

Consider these stated goals from WU and HIM:

"Students become part of a global apostolic family with a healthy foundation in apostolic authority and leadership. WU is all about seeing the fivefold ministry in Christ."[231]

And this under the title HIM leadership

---

[230] https://gloryofzion.org/about/
[231] https://wagner.university/#

218

"Each member of our leadership team is aligned with our vision and shares our desire to expand and grow the HIM network. All members function at the top of their sphere of influence and carry a distinctive heart for revival and reformation. Each member is prophetically chosen and recognized by the President and Presiding Apostle of HIM, Ché Ahn, to serve our global apostolic family.[232] *(Emphasis Mine)*

It is also important to remember that Doris Wagner is still around and is extremely influential in all these branches or networks. It is possible and likely that there is an understanding already regarding who is the Presiding Apostle, but that does not mean it will be publicly defined. These people are fine with secret councils and core leadership that is not explained to the public, and it makes for less public scrutiny.

Apostlemania

In 2019, Ché Ahn released a book titled, "Modern-Day Apostles: Operating in Your Apostolic Office and Anointing." This book and its timing are likely intended to solidify the movement and expand it. And since it comes from the Presiding Apostle over most branches of the movement, whether it is intended that way or not, it fills the vacuum left by Mr. Wagner. It is built on his teaching, except it is much bolder and presented as the correct teaching for all the church to embrace. And if you don't align with the modern apostles, which happens to be them, then you are illegitimate as a minister of Christ and are getting in the way of God's work. There is no other way to understand it. Honestly, the litany that appears in the table of contents is the most disturbing thing I think I have ever read. What arrogance, what chutzpah, what deception? Are you sitting down?

---

[232] https://www.harvestim.org/leadership/

Characteristics of a Modern-Day Apostle
Apostles are Called by God
Apostles are Sent by God
Apostles are Commissioned
Apostles Have Christlike Character
Apostles Have Extraordinary Authority
Apostles Have Authority to Wage Warfare and to Make Apostolic Decrees by Binding and Loosing
Apostles Have the Law of Apostolic Attraction
Apostles Are Aligned
Apostles Cast Vision
Apostles Work with Prophets
Apostles Form Apostolic Teams
There Are Many Different Types of Apostles
Apostles Are Revivalists: They are to Advance the Kingdom of Heaven with Signs and Wonders Following
Apostles are Catalytic Pioneers
Apostles Govern
Apostles Resolve Conflicts
Apostles Have Determined Spheres of Ministry
Apostles Receive Revelation[233]
Apostles Know How to Recognize, Disciple, and Raise up Leaders
Apostles Impart Spiritual Gifts

The Reformation Characteristics of an Apostle
Apostles Are Called to Disciple Nations with God's Word
Apostles Are Called to Bring God's Kingdom Culture to Earth
Apostles Are Kingdom-Hearted and Kingdom-Minded
Apostles Are Wise Master Builders
Marketplace Apostles are Aligned with Nuclear Apostles
Marketplace Apostles Have Respect

---

[233] This is the "Present Truth" they come up with, of course, New Bibles.

Apostles Have Money or Access to Wealth
Apostles Have Positions of Influence
Apostles Align the Generations
Apostles Know How to Finish

What you have just read is not a list of the characteristics of modern-day apostles. On the contrary, they actually serve the church and lay a foundation of Christ and not themselves. This is about ruling and reigning over God's people and the world like gods. With all due respect to Mr. Ahn, is there anything apostles can't do? I would like to know where the true apostles are because I am certain that a Biblical apostle would be confronting this and protecting the body of Christ.

NAR Bible

Then there is Brian Simmons, a close friend of Ahn's and faculty member of WU, who is also on the HIM leadership team. He came up with the "Passion Translation" (TPT) of the Bible, which he claims he got from a series of heavenly visits or trips where he also saw John Chapter 22.[234] The "Passion Translation" is quickly becoming the Bible for the Apostolic Movement even though it is filled with add on verses not in the actual Bible and translated with an allegorical and Replacement Theology bias and, of course, the agenda of the NAR. A critique of this false translation in itself would need much time and space. There are some splendid video critiques online along with the usual anti-Charismatic stuff.[235] Consider this quote from a Bible translator and scholar.

"Brian Simmons has made a new translation of the Psalms (and now the whole New Testament) which aims to 're-introduce the

---

[234] The gospel of John only contains 21 chapters.

[235] https://www.youtube.com/watch?v=CvllDpjVyCs

passion and fire of the Bible to the English reader.' He achieves this by abandoning all interest in textual accuracy, playing fast and loose with the original languages, and inserting so much new material into the text that it is at least 50% longer than the original. The result is a strongly sectarian translation that no longer counts as Scripture; by masquerading as a Bible it threatens to bind entire churches in thrall to a false god." [236]

Andrew G. Shead, is head of Old Testament and Hebrew at Moore Theological College, Sydney, and is a member of the NIV Committee on Bible Translation.

NAR Deniers

In this book, I have explained very clearly that the NAR, as it has come to be known, is not an organization in itself – it is a movement. Yet it is a movement that has many organizations and networks of accountability and the like, many of which are headed up by the same people. There are clear stated goals to which one must subscribe and requirements to be a member of these councils and fraternities including dues to be paid. Therefore, to deny the very existence of this movement is truly bizarre behavior indeed. It also raises an obvious question - why? Why the scurrying to distance oneself from an organization or a movement of organizations or churches? And why the angry and condescending responses? Could it really be that they are so ignorant of what the movement teaches or models and which their friends are all part of in one form or another? That is hard to imagine, though it is possible with some of these people. Nevertheless, they will declare they are merely ministers and friends and we are just conspiracy theorists. Well if that's true then give us a list of all the people in the inner councils and roundtables and secret meetings. No such things exist they say, and if they did, they certainly would not approve. Yet, a simple search on the web pages of their most trusted friends reveals

---

[236] https://www.thegospelcoalition.org/themelios/article/burning-scripture-with-passion-a-review-of-the-psalms-passion-translation

otherwise. Could the real reason for their acquiescence be the fact that all ministry doors would close should they confront anything within the NAR brotherhood? Perhaps you think that's extreme. But then how do you explain their vehement mocking denials and willingness to demonize anyone who exposes the teachings and practices of the movement? Surely this is the same kind of behavior one would expect from Bill Gates or Tony Fauci?

One such denier is Dr. Michael Brown who wrote an article in Charisma dated May 2018 titled, *"Dispelling the Myths About the New Apostolic Reformation."*[237] Here are some of his denials.

"To make matters more interesting, last year, some colleagues began sending me links to articles and videos attacking me as one of the leaders of NAR. Worse still, the websites claimed, I denied being part of it. How nefarious and dishonest of me! (To this moment, when I tell the truth about 'NAR,' I'm called a liar. It would be very funny if it wasn't very sad.) I began to ask other colleagues about NAR (or, in full, the New Apostolic Reformation). Almost to a person, they responded, "What is NAR?" Yet they, too, were alleged leaders in this so-called world movement! How is it they never heard of it either? (According to the critics, all of us are lying about our involvement in NAR because we're embarrassed by it. Honestly, these critics could make better use of their time writing a novel about the Illuminati.)"

"Dr. Wagner himself led something called the New Apostolic Reformation, and it was in that specific context I was familiar with the term. This was the 'NAR' I knew about. It had distinct teachings on apostolic ministry, some of which I agreed with and

---

[237] https://www.charismanews.com/opinion/in-the-line-of-fire/70844-dispelling-the-myths-about-the-new-apostolic-reformation

some of which I rejected. I was never part of the organization, which also had specific membership requirements and annual meetings.

To this day, when I bring up NAR to colleagues, either they have no idea what I'm referring to, or else they say, 'That was Peter Wagner's organization.'

I was having dinner recently with a well-known charismatic leader and asked him, 'What's the first thing that comes to mind when you think of NAR?'

He responded immediately with, 'It was a good attempt by Peter Wagner, but I strongly differed with him on a number of key points, which is why I never joined it.' (For the record, he was quite shocked when I told him that, according to the critics, he was also a major NAR leader!)

So, in this leader's mind, the New Apostolic Reformation spoke of something very specific, and that's how almost all of us who traveled in these same circles understood it. That's why we're scratching our heads today trying to understand how this term came to be used to describe this alleged worldwide, demonic movement. How in the world did this happen?"

Brown's argument is that the NAR was Peter Wagner's thing that he was doing but he and his colleagues disagreed with it and are not part of it. There is no doubt that the critics of the NAR who are non-charismatic lump all of us together and make many false assumptions which Brown easily exploits. Nonetheless, Dr. Brown's denial is also misleading and false. He then admits that one of his close friends and colleagues heads up this organization that Wagner started which, he denies has any real influence on him or the church as a whole.

"Recently, Dr. Joseph Mattera, who leads the organization once led by Peter Wagner, wrote two articles in which he strongly rejected some of the tenets of Wagner's NAR. But this doesn't matter to the critics. They simply heap scorn on him for being part of NAR and denying it. Do these critics really care about the facts?"

The problem with Dr. Brown's assertions is that they are completely false. How very convenient after Wagner's departure for him to distance Mattera from the NAR's lifetime Presiding Apostle, while at the same time admitting that his friend leads the organization founded by Peter Wagner. Indeed Joseph Mattera is the "convening apostle" of USCAL which is the American arm of ICAL. And Dr. Brown is a card-carrying member of this organization, as is clearly stated on ICAL's website.[238]

Prophetic Standards Statement
April 30, 2021

*Editors note: Charisma Magazine published the following article written by Jeff Struss on April 29, 2021. It explains why USCAL members, Michael Brown and Joseph Mattera (USCAL Convenor) constructed the **Prophetic Standards Statement**. Click for The Full Statement, including the initial signers - along with the opportunity to add your signature, if so desired.*

Furthermore, a 2017 list of USCAL council members has Michael Brown on it. This is a year before the Charisma article came out. Dr. Brown sits on a "council" with top ICAL members, who are not only aligned with each other, but pay hefty dues to be recognized as apostles or prophets. These are the real facts. Dr. Brown's denial of the NAR and his membership in it at the same time, is inexplicable. It can only be understood in the light of the NAR itself, and how good people who align with it come under

---

[238] https://www.icaleaders.com/news/2021/4/30/prophetic-standards-statement

a very strong delusion. Also, his assertion that his colleagues, who move in NAR circles as he does, do not promote Dominionism is absolutely false. One has only to read their writings which are all over the internet and clearly spelled out on the ICAL and USCAL and all the other NAR websites.

Daniel Kolenda

I must confess I know nothing about Daniel Kolenda other than that he took over the ministry of the well-respected Reinhard Bonnke. Nevertheless, in a recent podcast[239] he took issue with anyone who critiques the NAR, all of which in his ignorance he assumes are "Evangelical Heresy Hunters." Well with all due respect, it is clear he has no understanding of the message and structure of the movement. He refers to the 7 Mountain teaching as having come from Bill Bright and Loren Cunningham many years ago, as if somehow that makes it ok and mainstream. There is no "cabal" he says and nothing untoward going on. These are just Christians who want to change culture and make their political views known. They are not trying to take over the world or anything like that. But perhaps what was most disturbing were his claims that anyone who speaks out against the false teaching and practices of the NAR is influenced by liberals and working against Christ.

Mr. Kolenda means well but his comments are extremely naïve. The NAR does exist, and they do teach that the apostles are taking over the 7 Mountains and not just influencing them. Many of the key leaders are either Preterists or ardent Dominionists who believe the church has to come to a place of ruling and reigning in the earth before Jesus comes. They can publicly deny it, and they do. Yet their books and messages are available for all to read and study. Perhaps this is the most disturbing

---

[239] https://www.youtube.com/watch?v=BzcBsvnErkc&t=2873s

thing about the NAR is its doublespeak and cultlike refusal to accept any form of criticism. Instead they must always demonize those who challenge their teachings. Mr. Kolenda means well, but his association with top NAR apostles, and his brash foray into this issue, are a troubling sign for where his ministry is going. We can only pray that he and Dr. Brown and many like them, will come to their senses as this deeply flawed, man-centered movement continues to broaden its alliances and compromise the mission and message of the true gospel.

My update then concludes that the New Apostolic Reformation as defined by Peter Wagner is now mainstream for Charismatics and Pentecostals. This is precisely why people rush to defend it and deny its wild claims. In the last year, the Covid problem has made it harder for them to function. God is sifting and shaking everything. Nevertheless, all the evidence suggests that it will lead many Christians into the Harlot Church religious system of Revelation 17 – the state church that is now emerging which will receive a specific outpouring, not of the Holy Spirit, but of God's wrath.

Appendix
12 Obvious Reasons Preterism is False

1. Preterism is built on Replacement Theology. If Replacement Theology is false, so is Preterism. There are so many promises given to Israel, that have not yet been fulfilled or rescinded, and cannot be applied to the Church. The following are just a few:

"Thus says the LORD, who gives the sun for light by day, and the fixed order of the moon and the stars for light by night, who stirs up the sea so that its waves roar; the LORD of hosts is His name: 'If this fixed order departs from before Me,' declares the LORD. 'Then the offspring of Israel also will cease from being a nation before Me forever.'" Jer 31:35-36

"'Behold, I am going to make Jerusalem a cup that causes reeling to all the peoples around; and when the siege is against Jerusalem, it will also be against Judah. It will come about in that day that I will make Jerusalem a heavy stone for all the peoples; all who lift it will be severely injured. And all the nations of the earth will be gathered against it. In that day,' declares the LORD, 'I will strike every horse with bewilderment and his rider with madness. But I will watch over the house of Judah, while I strike every horse of the peoples with blindness. Then the clans of Judah will say in their hearts,' "A strong support for us are the inhabitants of Jerusalem through the LORD of hosts, their God."" Zech 12:2-5

"And I will set My glory among the nations; and all the nations will see My judgment which I have executed and My hand which I have laid on them. And the house of

Israel will know that I am the LORD their God from that day onward. The nations will know that the house of Israel went into exile for their iniquity because they acted treacherously against Me, and I hid My face from them; so I gave them into the hand of their adversaries, and all of them fell by the sword. According to their uncleanness and according to their transgressions I dealt with them, and I hid My face from them.'" Ezek 39:21-24

"For behold, in those days and at that time, when I restore the fortunes of Judah and Jerusalem, I will gather all the nations and bring them down to the valley of Jehoshaphat. Then I will enter into judgment with them there on behalf of My people and My inheritance, Israel, whom they have scattered among the nations; and they have divided up My land." Joel 3:1-2

2. In response to the question as to what was the sign of the "end of the age," Jesus said it was the Abomination of Desolation mentioned in Daniel. This was confirmed by Paul, as the occasion when the Antichrist literally sits in the Holy Place in Jerusalem, and proclaims himself God.[240] This sign is preceded, according to Jesus, by the preaching of the gospel to the whole world. How did this happen prior to 70AD, and when did the Antichrist take his seat in Jerusalem? Preterists say that Nero was the Antichrist. However, Nero never stood on the Temple Mount and declared himself God. He was a nutty despot, who burned Rome and used the occasion to enlarge his palace.

3. The Tribulation is described by Jesus as a time of such

---

[240] 2 Thess 2:3-4

distress, that there was never anything like it before, nor will there be again. He said that if it had not been cut short, no life would have been saved. The tribulation that Israel endured in 70AD, though it was horrendous for them, cannot be construed as a global event? Furthermore, if that was it, then there would not have been any event occurring afterwards, that could compare or cause more suffering. However, in the 20th Century alone, there were two world wars, where the toll of death and destruction was much greater. Fifty million died in World War II, not to mention the horrendous barbarism of the holocaust, and the Nuclear bombs dropped on Hiroshima and Nagasaki. Honestly, such a claim is insulting.

4. Jesus said in Luke 21:25-26 and Matthew 24:29-30 that there would be great signs at the end of the age, such as the sun becoming dark and the moon turning blood-red (not an eclipse), stars falling from the sky, the powers of the heavens shaken, and men fainting from fear because of the roaring of the sea and the waves (great tsunamis). If the end of the age took place in 70AD, then all these things should have taken place then.

5. According to Partial Preterists, Jesus came in the clouds in 70AD, pouring out wrath upon the Jews. If that were true, it would fulfill the following passages.

"And then the sign of the Son of Man will appear in the sky, and then all the tribes of the earth will mourn, and they will see the SON OF MAN COMING ON THE CLOUDS OF THE SKY with power and great glory. And He will send forth His angels with A GREAT TRUMPET and THEY WILL GATHER TOGETHER His elect from the

four winds, from one end of the sky to the other." Mt 24:30-31

"And I saw heaven opened, and behold, a white horse, and He who sat on it is called Faithful and True, and in righteousness He judges and wages war. His eyes are a flame of fire, and on His head are many diadems; and He has a name written on Him which no one knows except Himself. He is clothed with a robe dipped in blood, and His name is called The Word of God. And the armies which are in heaven, clothed in fine linen, white and clean, were following Him on white horses. From His mouth comes a sharp sword, so that with it He may strike down the nations, and He will rule them with a rod of iron; and He treads the wine press of the fierce wrath of God, the Almighty. And on His robe and on His thigh He has a name written, 'KING OF KINGS, AND LORD OF LORDS.'" Rev 19:11-16

"BEHOLD, HE IS COMING WITH THE CLOUDS, and every eye will see Him, even those who pierced Him; and all the tribes of the earth will mourn over Him. So it is to be. Amen." Rev 1:7

If these verses were fulfilled in 70AD, or any time close to that, then we must ask the following:
- When did all the tribes of the earth mourn for Jesus?
- When did the Jewish nation mourn over Jesus whom they had pierced?
- When did every eye see Him coming through the clouds?
- When did He gather the Jews from the four corners of the earth, or even Christians for that

matter?

- In 70AD Jerusalem was destroyed, and the Jews scattered. This was indeed, an outpouring of wrath as Jesus and the prophets predicted.[241] However, when it says that Jesus will come through the clouds with power and great glory, it says He will strike down the nations and fulfill the "great supper of God" prophecy of Ezekiel 39:17-20. When did this take place? Also, we are told that the Antichrist and the kings of the earth will make war against Jesus. When did this happen?

6. Jesus said that the end of the age would be like the days of Noah. The implication is clear, that people would be evil and clueless of the judgment that was coming. Then suddenly it came upon them, and they perished, but a remnant was delivered.

   "For as in those days before the flood they were eating and drinking, marrying and giving in marriage, until the day that Noah entered the ark, and they did not understand until the flood came and took them all away; so will the coming of the Son of Man be. Then there will be two men in the field; one will be taken and one will be left. Two women will be grinding at the mill; one will be taken and one will be left." Mt 24:38-41

   How can 70AD be compared to such a time for the nations, when they were, in fact, reveling in their victory over Zion? When did the destruction come upon them? Who were the ones rescued and snatched away from destruction? Furthermore, how can that time be

---

[241] Luke 21:22-24

considered more a fulfillment of the days of Noah than today? There is more evil on the earth today, like that of Noah's time, and Sodom and Gomorrah. Have the days of Noah come again, during the Millennium?

7. The Bible promises a bodily Resurrection at the end of the age.

"But as for you, go your way to the end; then you will enter into rest and rise again for your allotted portion <u>at the end of the age</u>." Dan 12:13 (Emphasis Mine)

"And I saw the souls of those who had been beheaded because of their testimony of Jesus and because of the word of God, and those who had not worshiped the beast or his image, and had not received the mark on their forehead and on their hand; and they came to life and reigned with Christ for a thousand years. The rest of the dead did not come to life <u>until the thousand years were completed.</u> This is the first resurrection." Rev 20:4-5 (Emphasis Mine)

Preterists say that the first Resurrection has already taken place, since they claim that the end of the age was 70AD. Thus, they deny the bodily resurrection promised at the end of this age, or say that it has already come and was not literal, but spiritual. How then can they escape the claim that their teaching is heretical?[242]

8. The Hebrew believers were told that Jesus would come again for them without reference to sin.[243] They were also

[242] 2 Tim 2:18
[243] Heb 9:28

told that they could see the day approaching.[244] Since Preterists say Jesus came in 70AD in judgment, and not without reference to sin, when were these verses fulfilled? And how could they be fulfilled in the future since there is no Day of the Lord approaching, and no signs.

9. Preterism depends on an early date for the Book of Revelation, yet, the testimony we have, says it was written in 95AD, during the time of Domitian.[245] Also, if it were not after the destruction of Jerusalem, how do we account for the time of worldwide persecution which sent John to exile on Patmos?

10. Preterists use Matthew 24:34 as a proof text to say that all the prophecies were fulfilled in the 1st Century. But they take the verse out of context, and ignore what they can't explain. Here is the verse in context:

"Now learn the parable from the fig tree: when its branch has already become tender and puts forth its leaves, you know that summer is near; so, you too, when you see all these things, recognize that He is near, right at the door. Truly I say to you, this generation will not pass away until all these things take place. Heaven and earth will pass away, but My words will not pass away." Mt 24:32-35

First of all, Jesus did not say that specific generation

---

would see it all, but the one than began to see the prophecies fulfilled. This is even clearer in Luke 21, where Jesus says, "when these things begin to take place."

"But when these things begin to take place, straighten up and lift up your heads, because your redemption is drawing near." Luke 21:28

Jesus clearly stated, that all that the Prophets had spoken would come to pass in the specific generation mentioned. If that was 70AD, then why did so many of the Prophets words not take place then? Examples are:

"For the earth will be filled with the knowledge of the glory of the LORD, as the waters cover the sea." Hab 2:14

"And the wolf will dwell with the lamb, and the leopard will lie down with the kid, and the calf and the young lion and the fatling together; and a little boy will lead them. Also the cow and the bear will graze; their young will lie down together; and the lion will eat straw like the ox. And the nursing child will play by the hole of the cobra, and the weaned child will put his hand on the viper's den. They will not hurt or destroy in all My holy mountain, for the earth will be full of the knowledge of the LORD as the waters cover the sea." Is 11:6-9

"And many peoples will come and say, 'Come, let us go up to the mountain of the LORD, to the house of the God of Jacob; that He may teach us concerning His ways, and that we may walk in His paths." For the law will go forth from Zion, and the word of the LORD from Jerusalem. And He will judge between the nations, and will render decisions for many peoples; and they will hammer their

swords into plowshares, and their spears into pruning hooks. Nation will not lift up sword against nation, and never again will they learn war. Come, house of Jacob, and let us walk in the light of the LORD." Is 2:3-5

Also, what redemption came for all believers in 70AD?

11. The events described by Paul, and referred to as the Day of the Lord, included the coming of Jesus for the Church in the Rapture, as well as the Abomination of Desolation.[246] Therefore, why did the Rapture of believers not occur in 70AD?

12. Peter, speaking of the Day of the Lord, said the following:

"But the day of the Lord will come like a thief, in which the heavens will pass away with a roar and the elements will be destroyed with intense heat, and the earth and its works will be burned up." 2 Pet 3:10

Did the elements melt with intense heat, like that of a nuclear blast, in 70AD? I don't think so. Furthermore, how could the cataclysmic events spoken of in Revelation have occurred in 70AD?

"And I looked when He broke the sixth seal, and there was a great earthquake; and the sun became black as sackcloth made of hair, and the whole moon became like blood; and the stars of the sky fell to the earth, as a fig tree casts its unripe figs when shaken by a great wind. And the sky was split apart like a scroll when it is rolled up; and every mountain and island were moved out of their places. And the kings of the earth and the great men

---

246 1 Thess 4:13 – 5:11, 2 Thess 2:1-12

and the commanders and the rich and the strong and every slave and free man, hid themselves in the caves and among the rocks of the mountains; and they said to the mountains and to the rocks, "Fall on us and hide us from the presence of Him who sits on the throne, and from the wrath of the Lamb; for the great day of their wrath has come; and who is able to stand?" Rev 6:12-17

Printed in Great Britain
by Amazon